DESIGNE

All those interested in stress management could gain a lot from this practical and helpful book.

John Collins, Chairman,
International Stress Management Association,
UK Branch
Stress News

. . . will be welcomed by those who have attended a SALT (Stress and Life Trust) seminar and also by the much wider public who have not had the opportunity of doing so.

Hugh Sansom
Healing and Wholeness

. . . may not only change your life, but extend your life.

Methodist Recorder

The emphasis is on action to be taken to survive in our stress-ridden culture, rather than merely understanding the problem. Bill Munro is a professional heavyweight.

Peter Meadows
Alpha

Easy to understand. Many will find the directive instructions in this handbook to be very helpful.

Ronald Messenger
Christian Herald

A practical handbook. Easy to read.

> June Chandler
> *Christian Counsellor*

A clear, straightforward address on the way to live above stress. Full of practical steps.

> June Boker
> *CiCP Newsletter*

A new, authoritative and very readable book on the way to beat stress.

> Olive Martin
> *ACT NOW*

Designer Living

The Way to Beat Stress

BILL MUNRO

STRESS AND LIFE TRUST
Bexhill

Copyright © Bill Munro 1991
The right of Bill Munro to be identified
as author of this work has been asserted by him in
accordance with the Copyright, Design
and Patents Act 1988

First published 1991
by Monarch Publications

This edition
published by SALT 1993

All rights reserved.
No part of this publication may be reproduced or
transmitted in any form or by any means, electronic
or mechanical, including photocopy, recording, or any
information storage and retrieval system, without
permission in writing from the publisher.

Unless otherwise indicated, biblical quotations are from the
Living Bible © Tyndale House Publishers, 1971. Use is
also made of the New International Version (NIV) © 1973,
1978, 1984 by The International Bible Society, and the
Authorised Version (AV) Crown copyright.

ISBN 0 9521583 0 2

Produced by Bookprint Creative Services
P.O. Box 827, BN23 6NX, England for
Stress And Life Trust (SALT)
The Istana, Freezeland Lane, Bexhill, E. Sussex, TN39 5JD.
Printed in Great Britain by Clay's Ltd, St Ives plc.
Typeset by J&L Composition Ltd, Filey, N Yorkshire

CONTENTS

Foreword	7
Acknowledgements	8
Introduction	9

Part One: Understanding Stress

1. What Is Stress?	13
2. Recognising Stress	17

Part Two: Beating Stress

3. Managing Stress	25
4. How Much Can I Take?	33
5. Support	41
6. Fitness	51
7. A Healthy Lifestyle	59
8. Your Self Image	69
9. Attitudes to Life	75
10. Perceptions	89
11. Practical Principles	95
12. The Spirit	101

Part Three: The Real Secret

13. Introduction to a Closed Book	109
14. Finding Support	113
15. Fit for Life	117

16. Changing Lifestyle 119
17. A New Identity 125
18. A Change of Attitude 131
19. Christian Thinking 135
20. Applying God's Principles 139

Part Four: Making It Work

21. A Change of Life 149

FOREWORD

The thought of a book on the psychology of stress can be quite daunting for ordinary mortals like us. But not so this book. It is compelling reading. It's layout is simple and straightforward, easy to read and very understandable, so that even those who are suffering from stress would not be intimidated by it's practical and commonsense approach.

The most exciting and important part of this book for us is Part Three, which grounds the whole topic of stress into the principles for Christian living, naming the Bible as the manual or handbook for life.

We have found, without exception, that abiding by these principles is the only way to keep ourselves fit to take on the stresses of life. For the Bible does not promise us a stress-free life, but the equipment to be fit for life whatever our circumstances.

But we are delighted to endorse the contents of *Designer Living* and we commend it to you, whether or not you are a Christian.

Psalm 34 v 8 reads: 'O taste and see that the Lord is good.' We encourage you to taste the contents of this book, which point to the maker's instructions—the only source of security and truth that will never let you down—and so discover how good the Lord is to those who trust him.

Roy and Fiona Castle

ACKNOWLEDGEMENTS

I would like to thank Sharon Butcher for her help with typing the original draft.

My wife, Frances, has been an invaluable source of inspiration and encouragement, as well as having spent many hours discussing drafts and retyping them, and I wish to express my deep appreciation for her.

INTRODUCTION

This book is about living successfully without fear of stress. You can be happier, more effective, nicer to know, and at peace with yourself and others. Developing the effects of stress at some time in your life is not inevitable, despite what you may have read, heard, been taught or believe.

If you are already suffering from the effects of stress or only just managing to cope, it is possible to free yourself from any further damage from stress and to start living a richly satisfying life. The life you lead, how you feel, think and behave, need not be dictated by your genes, your upbringing, circumstances, luck, or other people.

Is this too good to be true? Absolutely not! This book will show you valuable ways of managing your life so that you can reduce the pressures on yourself. It will also show you how you can become less vulnerable to the pressures you cannot avoid.

What you will learn is not just theory, but principles that I and my wife have found to work in our lives, and in the lives of many who have attended our seminars, and in those whom we have treated and counselled over the years. You too can live successfully, without fear of stress, if you follow the principles laid down in this book.

Part One

Understanding Stress

1
WHAT IS STRESS?

Before we can learn how to prevent or manage stress, we must be clear about what stress is, what causes it, and what makes it more likely that we will suffer from its effects.

Stressors

Anything which causes stress is called a 'stressor'.

A 'normal' stressor is an event or circumstance which challenges or excites us: physical danger, an examination, a competition, a race, a visit to the dentist, receiving bad news, a difficult interview, preparing for a big occasion, moving house, going on holiday, starting a new job, receiving a prize. 'Normal' stressors can be good or bad, planned or unplanned, and may involve changes in our life or circumstances.

The stress reaction

Faced with a stressor, the body reacts with a whole series of normal chemical, biochemical and hormonal changes. These bring about physical effects in the body, enabling us to perform better or to deal with the challenge: the so-called 'fight or flight' reaction. For example, our heart speeds up, our blood pressure goes up, and blood is diverted from our stomach to muscles and brain, to deliver more oxygen so that we can think faster and more clearly and act more decisively and strongly.

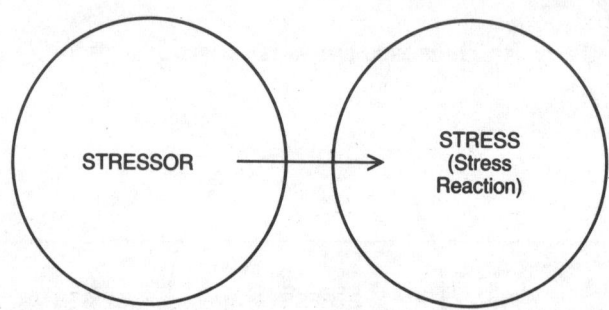

A pilot's heart rate is normally about 72 beats/min, but at take-off this can double. The same thing may happen to a racing driver's heart rate during the fastest and most difficult parts of a race. Some barristers, knowing that their hearts will pound in court, and actors whose pulses race on stage, take pills to slow their heart rate.

Our breathing gets faster and the airways open up so that we can take in the extra oxygen needed and get rid of carbon dioxide.

WHAT IS STRESS? 15

Our nervous system is stimulated and becomes more alert so that our reflexes become faster. Our brain is stimulated so that we can react more quickly. Our pupils dilate so that we can see as much as necessary. We sweat more so that our bodies will not overheat, and our blood becomes thicker so that if we are injured we will not bleed so quickly. Glycogen is turned into glucose, and triglycerides into free fatty acids to give us more energy.

When the stressor has ceased or has been dealt with—the examination over, the tooth filled, the race run—body chemistry and the physical changes return to normal, and the period of stress is over.

Strain

These stress reactions can have further effects on us—especially if we suffer them repeatedly. These effects are called 'strain'.

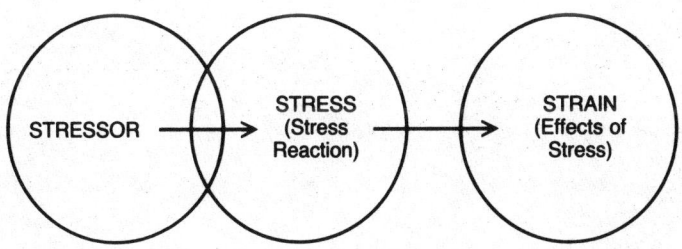

Problems can result when a stressor occurs very frequently (when we have daily rows with spouse or boss), or is just too great or overwhelming (if we are a victim or witness in a disaster), or goes on and becomes chronic (if we have to look after a handicapped child or ageing parent), or when a number of stressors hit us together or in close succession. We may be able to cope with pressure at work; but if in addition there are money worries at home and then illness strikes a member of the family, it can all become too much.

The stress reaction keeps going until either it becomes exhausted and we just cannot cope any more and feel like giving up, or the continuing changes begin to damage the body. This is when the effects of stress—or strain—begin to show. These can be vague to begin with and affect our feelings or behaviour. Often children are the first to know that Dad is under pressure as they become aware that he is bad tempered with them. We may begin to overreact to quite small problems. Later, mental problems, or psychosomatic conditions (associated partly with the mind and partly with the body), or physical conditions or illnesses, or spiritual problems can develop.

2
RECOGNISING STRESS

How can we tell if we are suffering from the effects of stress? Strain can produce a wide variety of symptoms.

Typical effects of stress–strain

Vague effects

Feeling down
  on edge
  irritable
  unreal
Crying easily
Wanting to run and hide
Difficulty in
  concentrating
  making decisions
Forgetting things
Putting things off
Fidgeting

Trembling
Sleeping badly
Nightmares
Fainting spells
Giddy spells
Nail biting
Stuttering
Racing pulse
Sweating easily
Difficulty in
  getting breath
  swallowing
Dry mouth

Lump in the throat
Loss of appetite
Excessive eating
Needing to urinate
Nervous laugh
Lack of sex drive
No energy
Easily tired
Easily startled by
  small noises
Impulsive behaviour
  (Prima donna)
Grinding teeth

Mental effects

Anxiety
Depression
Feeling helpless
  a failure
  like giving up
Nervous breakdown

Phobias
Panic attacks
Hysteria
Eating disorders
  bulimia, anorexia
  nervosa

Tension
Alcoholism
Increased smoking
Addictions
Hypochondria

17

Psychosomatic effects

Some forms of

Asthma	Backache	Diarrhoea
Hay fever	Neck pain	Premenstrual tension
Allergies	Shoulder pain	Dysmennorhoea
Eczema	Tinnitus	Impotence
Rashes	Spastic colon	Frigidity
Migraine	Irritable colon	Indigestion
Headaches	Constipation	Heartburn

Physical effects

High blood pressure	Lowered immunity	Chronic pain
Angina	Infections	Hormone problems
Ischaemic heart disease	Arthritis	Diabetes
Peptic ulcer	Cancer	Overactive thyroid

Spiritual effects

Dryness
Depression

Difficulty in praying
    going to church
    reading the Bible

Many of these conditions can be linked with other causes, but often they are stress-associated.

Ask yourself

Using the list of effects of stress–strain shown on p. 17, circle the numbers which best describe your experience in the last year.[1]

1 = none
2 = very slight
3 = slight
4 = moderate
5 = severe
6 = very severe

I have been experiencing:

(a) Vague effects of stress	1, 2, 3, 4, 5, 6
(b) Mental effects of stress	1, 2, 3, 4, 5, 6
(c) Psychosomatic effects of stress	1, 2, 3, 4, 5, 6
(d) Physical effects of stress	1, 2, 3, 4, 5, 6
(e) Spiritual effects of stress	1, 2, 3, 4, 5, 6
	Months in past year
(f) I have taken tranquillisers for	0 1 2 3 4 5 6
(g) I have taken sleeping pills for	0 1 2 3 4 5 6
	Times in past year
(h) I have consulted my GP for effects of stress	0 1 2 3 4 5 6
(i) I have seen a specialist for effects of stress	0 1 2 3 4 5 6

If you have scored many fours, fives or sixes and there is no physical cause, this suggests that you have been suffering from quite severe effects of stress–strain.

Scores in the mid-range, especially in categories (a) to (e), suggest mild to moderate degrees of strain.

Ideally, you should be scoring consistently at the low end of the scale.

High scorers—do not worry. By putting into action the principles in this book which apply to you, you can improve your score, and, more importantly your ability to live successfully without fear of stress.

Low scorers—good. By studying the principles in this book, you can keep in the low scores and live more successfully without fear of stress.

Helping others—you can help others deal with the effects of stress–strain by encouraging them to study and put into practice the principles which follow.

The size of the problem

It is estimated that the following are stress related:

more than 50% of all treated illness;
80% of all industrial accidents;
60% of company car accidents;

60% of absence from work—a staggering 40 million working days at a cost of £3,000 million.

The effects of stress cost ten times as much as all industrial disputes.

The Department of Employment estimates that alcohol abuse, often an effect of stress, costs British industry £700 million per year in lost output and sickness absence.

Almost 1 in 4 UK adults (about 10 million people) have taken tranquillisers at some time in their life.[2]

In a recent year, 1.8 billion tranquilliser tablets were prescribed—around 30 for every man, woman and child in the UK and costing £30 million.

Some 17% of all NHS medicines prescribed are 'mood altering'. This is the biggest category of all medicines prescribed.

The pressure/performance graph

This offers another way of looking at the effects of stressors:

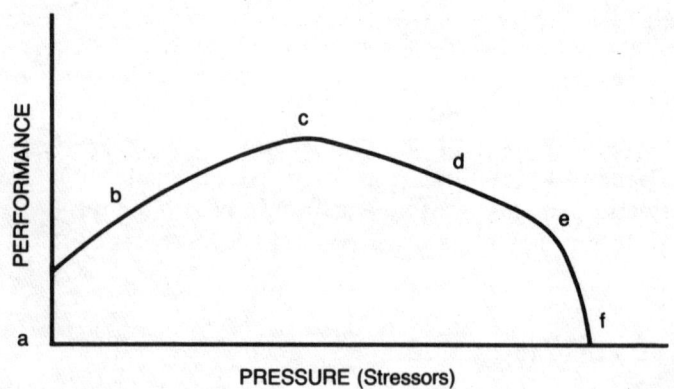

Point (a) where there is no pressure or no performance, is equivalent to being non-functional, or dead.

If there is too little pressure in our lives, and too little stimulation, then we are bored, around point (b).

As pressures increase for us (for instance, in sport), the bigger the occasion, the stiffer the opposition, the more our performance increases. An athlete often runs faster in the Olympic Games than he does in training where there is less pressure. Thus with increasing pressure performance increases and becomes optimum for the individual around point (c).

As pressures increase, however, performance does not go on up for ever in a straight line, but begins to level out. Fatigue, leading to exhaustion, develops when pressure is too great at around point (d).

With ever increasing pressure, at point (e), ill health comes on, and eventually performance ceases almost totally at (f), breakdown.

Where are you on the pressure/performance graph? By putting into practice the principles I will explain later, you can remain consistently around point (c).

Notes

1. Taken from *Stress Facts and Action Plan*, Bill Munro, Stress and Life Trust (SALT) 1989.
2. MORI Poll 1984.

Part Two

Beating Stress

3
MANAGING STRESS

My wife and I spend much of our time counselling people or conducting seminars for people who are suffering from the effects of stress; many have been helped by applying the principles in this book. But prevention is even better, and so we run seminars for people who want to know how to avoid the effects of stress and live life to the full.

All of what follows applies to both prevention and management of stress. Some principles and factors may be more applicable than others to any one individual but all should be checked out and reviewed.

Important—if you believe you are suffering from conditions which may be effects of stress, it is very important before going further that you consult your doctor, so that any physical causes of your symptoms can be excluded. Having done this, you can then proceed to study the information on beating stress in this section, and to put into action the advice which applies to you.

Identifying stressors

The first step in the prevention or management of stress is to review the stressors or external pressures in your life. This helps to clarify where the problems lie, and focus on the source or potential source of the stress rather than on the effects.

Sometimes it is easy to identify a big stressor, but there may also be a number of lesser stressors associated with it or which go to make it up. For instance, the stressor may be that you are looking after an ageing relative. But what are the specific factors within this overall big stressor which are the real stressors? Or the major stressor may be work. But this must be broken down and analysed so that the actual factors at work causing the problem can be identified.[1,2]

David, a young executive in a company, came to see me recently because he had developed headaches and was not sleeping well. A full physical examination revealed no abnormalities, and his symptoms sounded like early and vague effects of stress. Most of his life was in good shape but he was not enjoying his work. He was anxious about it. We sat down and explored the usual work stressors.

He was certainly working hard but not excessively so. He had deadlines to meet but usually he met them without too much of a problem. So we could rule out *overwork, underwork* and *pressure of deadlines*.

There was no *conflict* in the job he was doing—that is, he was not being pulled in more than one direction or being asked to try to achieve two conflicting and incompatible goals. This kind of role conflict can arise, for example, in personnel departments where staff are expected to be and want to be caring, but at the same time they are expected to be tough, impose discipline and even fire people where necessary.

His company was a good ethical one and he was not being asked to do anything which he felt uncomfortable with or was in any way dishonest. The goods he sold were good, so that he did not have to exaggerate their claims and worth, so *moral issues* as a stressor could be ruled out.

As in all companies there were *office politics*, but they

were not excessive and he had not been drawn into them too much. So again, this was not a big stressor in his case. He had been in his present job for about two years, so he had settled down and was not having to contend with a new job, nor had he recently had a change of house. He had a very short distance to travel to work, so that pressures of a *new job, moving house* and *commuting* could be put aside.

The company was stable, was profitable and there were no rumours of mergers, takeovers or other changes so there was no *uncertainty* as far as a continuing job was concerned. These, together with privatisation, nationalisation, and rationalisation are very big stressors in some businesses nowadays and are increasing. Many companies insist on more productivity, more efficiency and more work from fewer people in longer hours, so that pressures on employees and managers continue to increase.

The company was involved in light industry, situated in a pleasant coastal area, and David had a nice office so that there were no *environmental stressors*. There was some development of *new technology* within the company which did affect David, but he was very capable and this was not a problem.

So far we were drawing a blank, but David insisted that the big stressor in his life was his work.

As we probed further I found that while his *relationships* with his colleagues were good, he felt ill at ease with his boss. There had been no rows, no criticism of what he had been doing, but he still felt vaguely insecure as far as his boss was concerned. He was not very sure what the next step in his career would be. But most of all, while he was working hard and his boss seemed pleased with what he did, or at least had not criticised him, David was not absolutely sure what he was supposed to be striving for in his job, what was really expected of him, what his limits of authority were, and what he would be judged on.

This *role ambiguity*, as it is called, is a very big stressor because of its very uncertainty. David could soon see that this was indeed the big stressor at work, which was causing him problems.

How he dealt with it we shall see presently, but even now we can see that it is not enough to say 'the stressor is work'; you have to analyse the apparent stressor to establish what the real culprit is before you can deal with it, and you may need help in this analysis and identification.

A plan of action

The next step is to face the stressors and consider if they can be discontinued, reduced, or dealt with in some other way. Then take action.

Having established that *role ambiguity* was the big stressor, what could and should David do about it?

A ship in a storm does best if it turns into the wind, but continues to be vulnerable if it turns side on. Or to change the metaphor, the ostrich solution is not recommended: do not try to ignore the problem, hoping it will go away. In our experience, unresolved conflict is one of the biggest and worst stressors around. Nor is the geographic cure—moving job, house, area—usually the best solution. The stressor may follow you, or similar ones arise in the new environment. Having said that, drastic means are sometimes necessary, and on occasion, people have thrown everything up and moved successfully to the Outer Hebrides.

While David felt better just knowing the cause of his strain, he decided that he should not ignore the situation, or hope that it would go away or improve. Equally, there was no need at this stage for him to look for another job. He would face the stressor straight on.

We discussed the possibilities and it seemed that the best would be for David to ask for an interview with his boss. He would be quite open with him and explain that he was not sure what exactly was expected of him. He would ask his boss for guidance and clarification about the whole area of his job, overall responsibilities, his longer-term and short-term goals and what his boss would like to see in terms of achievements. At the same time he would broach the subject of career development as his boss saw it.

The outcome, I was pleased to find out, was that David's boss was able to flesh out David's job description with him and David has felt much better since the interview and is once again secure and happy in his job. His relationship with his boss has improved and David feels that his boss seemed to quite welcome David's approach to him and the opportunity to discuss what he felt should be David's goals.

Avoidable stressors

It is particularly important also that you ruthlessly deal with any self-inflicted stressors.

Dishonest or questionable practices in work or business can bring guilt and a constant fear of being found out—a continuing stressor working away just below the surface. If you are in this situation then you need to acknowledge these practices, right whatever wrongs need righting, make restitution where necessary and decide to act honestly and openly in future.

If too big or too many financial commitments are a continuing stressor in your life, especially when the monthly bank statement comes in or bills become due, then you should consider whether all your commitments are necessary. Did you get into them because of trying to keep up with the Joneses? Or merely because you succumbed to the easy credit, live today and pay tomorrow, propaganda? What can be done to reduce them? The answer may seem drastic sometimes. Plastic surgery—cutting up your credit cards—may be necessary. You may even have to consider moving house if your mortgage is too large: a difficult option when interest rates are high and few buyers are around, but better surely to live without such a large and insistent stressor, no matter what it takes.

Irresponsible action, gambling, heavy drinking, poor housekeeping, laziness—all these can be stressors in the family, leading to effects of stress in individual family members and sometimes, ultimately, break-up of the family. If you know that your actions are irresponsible and potent stressors, acknowledge them and find ways of changing them.

The thought of a secret love affair may have attractions in the early stages—excitement, attention, a new zest for life—but if we give in to the temptation and commit adultery, stress results. Guilt and fear of discovery are powerful stressors and, if events proceed, stressors surround the divorce—lawyers, court appearances, dealing with the children and so on. I wonder how many would have started the flirtation with what appeared a harmless friendship, had they known the ultimate cost in stressors and their effects. Breaking off an illicit relationship, although a stressor itself, will prevent an ongoing and chronic stressor which may lead to more or greater stressors in the long run.

There is, I believe, good ambition—but overambition, when ambition becomes all-consuming, can lead to too much time at the office and on business trips. How often do we hear of a man whose business is ultra-successful but whose children or wife have become disillusioned and difficult or ill or whose family life is a disaster? Decisions have to be made to prevent such a catastrophe or the situation retrieved.

You may be saying, 'I cannot avoid the stressors in my life and cannot do anything about them.' There are indeed such stressors which cannot be avoided or changed and we will deal with the answer to this later. However, it is not always easy to identify the real stressors and, even if we do, there is a tendency then, without further thought, to dismiss any possibility of being able to do anything about them. This particularly applies to stressors which we are not willing to admit that we have brought on ourselves; the self-inflicted stressors. 'The job requires sixty hours work per week and periods away from home.' 'I could not be completely honest or I would not make my sales targets.' 'I have to do it all myself. I cannot ask anyone to help.'

We do not like to think that we have shot ourselves in the foot rather than being honourably wounded; we do not like to think that we have scored an own goal. We would rather believe that we have had to contend with terrific odds and have had no chance of winning through; indeed, we may have been beaten unfairly. But if we are brutally frank and honest, have these stressors all been inevitable and unavoidable?

We would strongly recommend that you enlist the help of a trusted friend who will be open and honest with you—or better still, a professional counsellor—to help identify and analyse the stressors in your life and then to help you honestly to see whether anything can be done about them and what that might be.

Summary

The first steps in stress prevention and management.

1. Identify the stressors (external pressures) in your life.
2. Decide what can be done to remove, change or reduce these stressors.

3. Do this with the help of someone you can trust, or with a trained counsellor.

Notes

1. Caplan, R. D., et al. (1975) *Job Demands and Worker Health*. HEW Publication No N10SH 75–160, Washington, DC.
2. Cooper, C. L. and Paynne, R. (eds) (1978) *Stress at Work*. Wiley, New York.

4

HOW MUCH CAN I TAKE?

From the cradle to the grave, life is full of stressors. Some are bigger than others.

Shakespeare wrote about some of these in his 'Seven Ages of Man'. Being born is stressful, as mothers know, and dads who have been present at the birth of their children; starting school, coping with exams, with homework, with bullies, with competition and rejection and failure are all stressful; adolescence has its own stressors in growing up, and going to university or college or starting work are others; getting married, adjusting to married life, having children and bringing them up all can be very stressful; job changes and fear of redundancy or unemployment go on throughout working life; retirement can result in financial pressure, loss of identity and status; old age brings with it infirmities, failing health and loss of vigour; and sometimes fear of death completes the stressors of normal life.

Grading stressors

A number of studies have graded the severity of life stressors and their relationship to disease.[1-14] Some years ago, Drs Holmes and Rahe found that the death of a husband or wife is likely to have the biggest effect on us.[15] This stressor has been given a score of 100 (see p.

34). Things like being sacked at work and trouble with in-laws affect us less, and they have been given scores of 47 and 29 respectively. Even going on holiday, although good for us, can create stress in a number of ways: getting everything ready, getting to the station or airport on time, travel delays, hotels and rooms not up to expectations, upset stomachs, poor weather, and so on. Holidays register a score of 13. Christmas, usually thought of as a happy time of the year, can be a stressful period for families as many of us know; it has been given a score of 12.

These scores are averages and will not apply exactly to everyone. Although pregnancy is given a score of 40, it is likely to be more stressful for a young unmarried girl, who does not want the baby, than for a couple who have planned to have one, although for both it is stressful. People who work in the Post Office find Christmas, their busiest time of the year, more stressful than others do.

The stress of adjusting to change

(This list is based on Drs Holmes & Rahe, 1967)

Events	Scale of impact
Death of spouse	100
Divorce	73
Marital separation	65
Jail term	63
Death of close family member	63
Personal injury or illness	53
Marriage	50
Fired at work	47
Marital reconciliation	45
Retirement	45
Change in health of family member	44
Pregnancy	40
Sex difficulties	39
Gain of new family member	39

Business readjustment	39
Change in financial state	38
Death of close friend	37
Change to different line of work	36
Change in number of arguments with spouse	35
Large mortgage	31
Foreclosure of mortage or loan	30
Change in responsibilities at work	29
Son or daughter leaving home	29
Trouble with in-laws	29
Outstanding personal achievement	28
Wife begins or stops work	26
Begin or end school	26
Change in living conditions	25
Revision of personal habits	24
Trouble with boss	23
Change in work hours or conditions	20
Change in residence	20
Change in schools	20
Change in recreation	19
Change in church activities	19
Change in social activities	18
Small mortgage or loan	17
Change in sleeping habits	16
Change in number of family get-togethers	15
Change in eating habits	15
Vacation	13
Christmas	12
Minor violations of the law	11

The more points we amass over a short period, the more likely we are to suffer from some of the effects of stress. For example, if we run up a score of more than 300 quickly—say in six months or so—then there may be an 80% chance of us being ill in the next few months. With a score of 150–299 there may be a 50% chance and so on.

Who succumbs to stress?

We have just seen that the bigger the stressor score the more chance we have of suffering from strain (ie the effects of stress).

One morning recently, I was asked to see a man and give an opinion about his fitness for certain work. It appeared that he had not worked for fourteen years. He was reluctant to tell me why, but I had to press him in case he had had some severe illness or disease which might affect his ability now. In confidence he told me that he had been in jail for murdering his wife.

We can imagine the kind of pressures on this man. The memory of what he had done, the guilt, the scars from years in prison, the suspicion when he looked for work and prospective employers learned his story, the frustration at not finding work. We should perhaps not be surprised if someone like this, facing quite overwhelming stressors, were to suffer from the effects of stress.

That same afternoon, I was asked to see a young lady about her fitness to work. She too had gone through a period of extreme pressure. The man she had been living with was murdered in front of her eyes. She was blamed by his parents and had to leave the area, so she moved to the south coast where she knew no one and was lonely. Eventually, she met and started living with another man, but soon afterwards he was sent to prison for fraud. She visited him in prison and one year ago they had been married in a prison ceremony. Now she was very apprehensive about his coming release. Again, one can hardly be surprised if this young lady were to suffer from anxiety and phobias and other effects of stress because of the overwhelming stressors she has faced.

However, we all know people who have had a number of really big stressors in their lives but have come through them with no sign of a nervous breakdown or

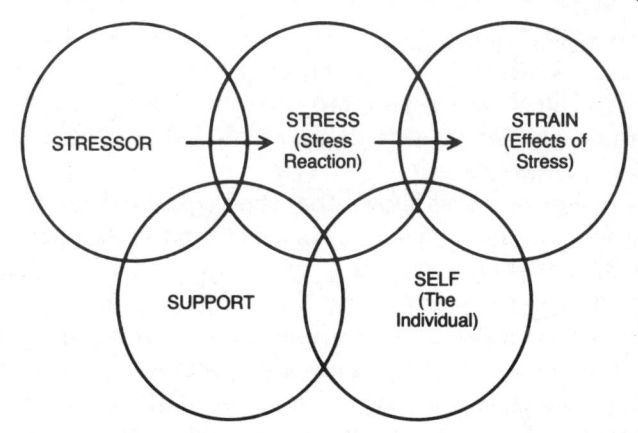

```
                STRESS                STRAIN
STRESSOR  →    (Stress      →       (Effects of
                Reaction)             Stress)


                            SELF
        SUPPORT             (The
                            Individual)
```

other illness. On the other hand, some people develop the effects of stress although they have had comparatively small stressors to cope with. Why is this?

Stress researchers have become more interested in this recently, and they have come up with two principal factors which seem to account for these differences. These factors act as moderators or mediators of stressors and, to a large extent, determine how badly or how well we will respond to the stressors that are present in our lives.

The first moderator is support: contact with some external source of comfort or help which protects us or strengthens us to face difficulties. The second stress moderator is self, or the individual: there are some elements of personality and lifestyle which affect how we respond to stress.

Clearly, if we can find sufficient external support from family, friends, doctors or ministers, then we are more likely to survive stressors and emerge unharmed. We shall look at some possible forms of support in the next chapter.

However, stressors can be devastating, and support almost non-existent, yet some individuals seem to cope so well that they do not suffer from the effects of stress. In other cases the stressors are only ordinary and there is a good deal of support around, yet some individuals cannot cope and seem to suffer immediately from the effects of stress.

Current research shows that the biggest moderator of stressors is the individual himself. What is it about the individual that makes this difference? Why are some individuals more and some less vulnerable to stress? A number of factors make the difference and if we can learn from them, then we can protect ourselves from the effects of stress. In Chapters 6–12 we shall look at these characteristics and see how we can develop them.

Notes

1. SELYE, H. (1956) *The Stress of Life*. McGraw-Hill, New York.
2. HINKLE, L. E. and WOLFF, H. G. (1958) 'Ecologic investigations of the relationship between illness, life experiences and the social environment'. *Ann. Intern. Med.* 49: 1373.
3. RAHE, R. H. (1968) 'Life-change measurement as a predictor of illness' *Proc. Roy. Soc. Med.*, 61: 1124.
4. PAYKEL, E. S., MYERS, J. K., DIENELT, M. N. et al. (1969) 'Life events and depression: A controlled study'. *Arch. Gen. Psychiatry* 21: 753.
5. PAYKEL, E. S., PRUSOFF, B. A. and UHLENHUTH, E. H. (1971) 'Scaling of life events'. *Arch. Gen. Psychiatry* 25: 340.
6. THEORELL, T. and RAHE, R. H. (1971) 'Psychosocial factors and myocardial infarction. An inpatient study in Sweden'. *J. Psychosom. Res.* 15: 25.
7. THEORELL, T. and RAHE, R. H. (1972) 'Behavior and life satisfactions characteristic of Swedish subjects with myocardial infarction'. *J. Chron. Dis.* 25: 139.
8. DOBSON, C. B. (1982) *Stress: The hidden adversary*. Lancaster Medical and Technical Publishers.
9. KAPLAN, H. B. (1983) *Psychosocial stress: Trends in theory and research*. Academic Press, New York.

10. JENKINS, C. D. (1983) 'Psychosocial and behavioral factors' in *Prevention of coronary heart disease*. N. Kaplan and J. Stamler, (eds), Saunders, Philadelphia.
11. COOPER, C. L. (1983) *Stress research*. Wiley, New York.
12. COOPER, C. L. (1984) *Psychosocial stress and cancer*. Wiley, New York.
13. WELLS, J. A. (1985) 'Chronic life situations and life change events' in *Measuring psychosocial variables in epidemiologic studies of cardiovascular disease*. N.I.H., Bethesda, M.D.
14. GLASER, R., KIECOLT-GLASER, J. K., STOUT, J. C., TARR, K. L., SPEICHER, C. E. and HOLLIDAY, J. E. (1985) 'Stress-related impairments in cellular immunity'. *Psychiatric Res*. 16: 233.
15. HOLMES, T. G. and RAHE, R. H. (1967) 'The social readjustment rating scale' *J. Psychosom. Res*. 11: 213.

5
SUPPORT

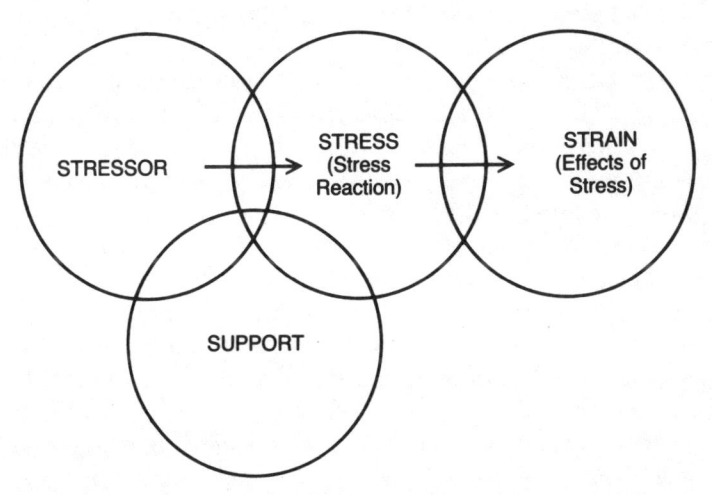

```
STRESSOR → STRESS (Stress Reaction) → STRAIN (Effects of Stress)
                    SUPPORT
```

Studies have shown that those who get adequate support—physical, moral, psychological or spiritual—when it is needed are less likely to suffer from the effects of stress.[1-24] For example, in one study it was shown that unemployed workers who had little or no support from family, friends or social networks were more likely to suffer from mental and physical illness than those who had support available.[25] It is important, therefore, if you want to prevent or manage stress, that you make use of as much support as you can get.

Family support

Much support used to be available from the family and, if you have an understanding family available, then this is often the first place to look for support. Heart disease in Japanese living in the USA is more likely than in Japanese living in Hawaii, and the rate there is higher than in Japanese still living in Japan. These differences are not accounted for simply by differences in things like smoking habits and diet. The differences are put down to the presence or absence of family support, it being greatest in Japan and least in USA.[26]

Husbands who get good support from their wives may be less likely to suffer from a heart attack, and one recent study demonstrated this indirectly.[27] So wives, if you want your husbands to stay healthy and not have a premature heart attack, it is important to back them up and support them at every turn and in every way.

Wives whose husbands show love and affection seem less likely to feel rejected and depressed. So husbands, if you want a healthy, happy wife who is going to support you at every turn, it is important to tell her, and show her, that you love her.

Where wives respect and support their husbands, and husbands love and cherish their wives, there are fewer pressures in the marriage; the marriage is more stable and fewer effects of stress are experienced by both partners. Receiving love or 'TLC' (tender loving care) has quite a marked effect on us. Amongst other things it reduces our blood cholesterol level and this protects us from premature furring up of the arteries and a heart attack. Studies have shown that children thrive and grow up much better if they receive plenty of love.

In a recent study, in a maternity hospital in Guatemala, half of the women in labour were allocated a lay helper to stay with them, talk with them, and rub their backs and generally support them during this stressful time. Results of this study were quite amazing. Those who had a helper were likely to have a shorter labour, fewer complications, were more awake after delivery and bonded better with their children.[28]

This study was repeated with much larger numbers of women with similar results.[29]

Other sources of support

Support may be available from the NHS or Social Services or from voluntary organisations, but often nowadays all these services are so stretched that there may be a long waiting list, or the particular help needed may simply be unavailable locally.

If you work you may be fortunate in having support available there from management, from colleagues, from the welfare department or the occupational health service. A recent study showed that female clerical workers who got no support from their supervisors were more likely to suffer from heart disease than those who could count on support.[30]

Good friends can be an excellent source of support.

However, sometimes family, friends, and work are not sources of support, tender loving care or love, and you may have found other sources wanting. If you are not a church goer, have you thought of looking for a supportive church?

Many of us, unfortunately, are too proud and too self-sufficient to admit that we need support, and so we go on trying to manage on our own—sometimes until things have got so bad that we really are suffering from the effects of stress. When support is offered, we are too proud or stubborn to accept it until, in the end, we have no choice but to accept it.

The false supports

Some things seem as if they are giving us support when we start using them—like alcohol, smoking, drugs, and food, especially high carbohydrate foods—but they soon let us down. They ruin our health and soon we need to increase our consumption of them and become addicted, which only increases our problems. When we do realise that we are worse off with them, we find it extremely difficult to stop, and we may suffer tremendous withdrawal symptoms. It is better not to start.

Advice about alcohol

It is almost certain that if alcohol were submitted to the authorities today as a medicine, it would be turned down because of its toxicity. It damages the liver. It kills brain cells and when brain cells are dead, they cannot recover.

Large quantities of alcohol will damage health. Even quite small quantities affect both behaviour and judgement, and so we should be careful about any alcohol. However, in times of relaxation, a little alcohol—say a glass of wine or a measure of gin or whisky or a beer—is not harmful and, in fact, may be quite beneficial for health and especially for the arteries and heart.

There are many misconceptions about drinking alcohol; for example, that wine is less harmful than beer and beer is less harmful than the hard stuff. This is wrong. It is the amount of alcohol in the drink which counts and, in general terms, 1 glass of wine = 1 small short = 1 sherry = $\frac{1}{2}$ pint of beer.

Another misconception is that a little alcohol will not affect judgement and can even improve it. In fact, even a little alcohol can affect our judgement and reflexes; it is important to avoid it when we have to drive or make importance decisions.

Alcohol also affects your sex life. Our professor of pharmacology used to tell us: 'Alcohol increaseth the desire but taketh away from the performance.'

One of the great dangers of alcohol is the possibility of becoming addicted to it; you should be very careful to avoid increasing amounts or increasing use.

Warnings about smoking

While we have seen that a little alcohol is probably quite good for you, the same does not apply to smoking. *Any* smoking is bad for you and there is really only one thing to be said about smoking—'Don't.'

The saying, 'I'm dying for a smoke' is very apt. Not only is smoking the main cause of cancer of the lung, it is also one of the main factors in emphysema and chronic bronchitis, and smokers are much more liable to have heart attacks. It has now also been incriminated in cancer of the cervix.

Smokers sometimes say, 'But it's my choice, and if I choose to take the risk then that is my business.' This is not so. It is now known that passive smoking, ie, inhaling the smoke of others, can damage the health: it is only a matter of time before smoking will be banned in all public places. Employers are now recognising that their employees should be able to ask for smoke-free working conditions. Employers, indeed, are obliged by law to provide a healthy and safe environment for their employees; again, it is only a matter of time before a test case arises. Either an employee will ask for and be refused a no-smoking office, and then take the employer to court, or an employee will become ill through passive smoking and sue an employer for not providing a healthy and safe environment.

If you do not smoke: good—do not start. But beware of passive smoking.

If you do smoke, do try to stop. There are a number of methods and organisations offering help. If you do continue to smoke, however, do not be selfish by forcing others to inhale your smoke, damage their health, and pollute their hair and clothes. It is particularly important that you do not affect your children's or grandchildren's health by your smoking. Pregnant women who smoke can damage their unborn baby in the womb.

Smoking appears to increase face wrinkles so that is perhaps another reason why women should not smoke. It also affects men's sex life—another reason for men to avoid it.

While cigarettes are the worst form of smoking, cigars and pipes carry risks too, especially if the smoke is inhaled.

Warnings about tranquillisers

It is now realised that some types of tranquillisers prescribed by doctors, especially those of the benzodiazepine family, (often those with names ending with '... pam') can have very disturbing side effects. Occasionally these effects are worse than the original anxiety for which the pills were prescribed. They can also be highly addictive, causing great problems when they are withdrawn. The Department of Health warned doctors in the United Kingdom in 1988 that these tranquillisers should be prescribed only with great care, and only if the condition of the patient was really bad enough to warrant it. One eminent professor of psychiatry in the UK has said that they should never be prescribed. I have had to deal with a number of patients who needed much help, support and counselling when they were trying to wean themselves off these medicines.

Someone has said that taking tranquillisers is like turning off the fire bell because you do not like the noise it is making. Instead, take the anxious feelings as a warning. Look for help and deal with the causes. If a red warning light appears on the dashboard of your car, you are unwise to cover it up, or to try to turn it off. It is there to warn you that something is wrong, that you should slow down, seek help, and have the cause traced and dealt with.

Beware of overeating

It is easy to begin comfort eating when you are anxious or under pressure. If this becomes a habit, it can lead to an unhealthy gain in weight.

Summary

Support is an important moderator of stressors and helps us to contend with stressors in our lives.

1. Look for and accept as much support and love as you can, from whatever good source is available—family, friends, doctors, NHS, Social Services, counsellor, pastor, minister, church members, housegroup members.
2. If you are in a position to give support or love, then you should do so, and you will help others to withstand the pressures that they have to face.
3. Do not rely on alcohol, tobacco or benzodiazepine tranquillisers, or overeating.

Notes

1. MEDALIE, J., SNYDER, M., GROEN, J. J. et al. (1973) 'Angina pectoris among 10,000 men: five year incidence and univariate analysis'. *Am. J. Med.* 55: 583.
2. CASSEL, J. (1974) 'Psychosocial processes and stress: Theoretical formulations'. *Int. J. Health Services* 4: 471.
3. BERKMAN, L. F. and SYME, S. L. (1979) 'Social networks, host resistance and mortality: A nine year follow-up study of Alameda county residents'. *Am. J. Epidemiol.* 109: 186.

4. VACHON, M. L. S., LYALL, W. A. L., ROGERS, J., FREEDMAN-LETOFSKY, K. and FREEDMAN, S. J. (1980) 'A controlled study of self-help intervention for widows'. *Am. J. Psychiatry* 137: 1380.
5. GOTTLIEB, B. H. (ed.) (1981) *Social Networks and Social Support*. Sage, Beverley Hills, C.A.
6. HOLOHAN, C. J. and MOOS, R. H. (1981) 'Social support and psychological distress: A longitudinal analysis'. *J. Abnormal Psychol.* 49: 365.
7. WILLIAMS, A. W., WARE, J. E. and DONALD, C. A. (1981) 'A model of mental health, life events and social support applicable to general populations'. *J. Health Soc. Behav.* 22: 324.
8. BLAYER, D. G. (1982) 'Social support and mortality in an elderly community population'. *Am. J. Epidemiol.* 115: 684.
9. DEAN, A. and ENSEL, W. M. (1982) 'Modelling social support, life events, competence and depression in the context of age and sex'. *J. Community Psychol.* 10: 392.
10. HOUSE, J. S., ROBBINS, C. and METZNER, H. (1982) 'The association of social relationships and activities and mortality: Prospective evidence from the Tecumseh community health study'. *Am. J. Epidemiol.* 116: 123.
11. KASL, S. V. and COBBS, S. (1982) 'Variability of stress effects among men experiencing job loss' in *Handbook of stress*. L. Golderger and S. Breznitze (eds) Free Press, New York.
12. ROSKIN, M. (1982) 'Coping with life changes—A preventive social work approach'. *Am. J. Community Psychol.* 10: 331.
13. BERKMAN, L. F. and BRESLOW, L. (1983) *Health and ways of living: Findings from the Alameda County Study*. Oxford University Press, New York.
14. BROADHEAD, W. E., KAPLAN, B. H., SHERMANN, S. A., WAGNER, E. H., SCHOENBACH, V. G. and GEHLBACH, S. H. (1983) 'The epidemiological evidence between social support and health'. *Am. J. Epidemiol.* 117(5): 521.
15. GOTTLIEB, B. H. (ed.) (1983) *Social Support Strategies*. Sage, Beverley Hills, C.A.

16. REED, D., McGEE, D., YANO, K. and FEINLEIB, M. (1983) 'Social networks and coronary heart disease among Japanese men in Hawaii'. *Am. J. Epidemiol.* 117: 384.
17. RUBERMAN, W., WEINBLATT, E., GOLDBERG, D. D. and CHANDBURY, B. (1986) 'Psychosocial influences on mortality after myocardial infarction'. *N. Eng. J. Med.* 311: 552.
18. BERKMAN, L. F. (1985) 'The relationship of social networks and social support to morbidity and mortality' in *Social Support and Health*. S. Cohen and L. Syme (eds) Academic Press, New York.
19. COHEN, S. and WILLS, T. A. (1985) 'Stress, social support, and the buffering hypothesis'. *Psychol. Bull.* 2: 310.
20. COHEN, S. and SYME, S. L. (eds) (1985) *Social Support and Health*. Academic Press, New York.
21. KASL, S. V. and WELLS, J. A. (1985) 'Social support and health in the middle years' in *Social Support and Health*. S. Cohen and L. Syme (eds) Academic Press, New York.
22. CASPI, A., BOLGER, N. and EOKENRODE, J. (1987) 'Linking person and context in the daily stress process'. *J. Pers. Soc. Psychol.* 52: 184.
23. ROOSE, P. E. and COHEN, L. H. (1987) 'Sex roles and social support as moderators of life stress adjustments'. *J. Pers. Soc. Psychol.* 52: 576.
24. GANSTER, D. C. and VICTOR, B. (1988) 'The impact of social support on mental and physical health'. *Br. J. Med. Psychol.* 61: 17.
25. GORE, S. (1978) 'The Effects of social supports in moderating the health consequences of unemployment'. *J. Health & Soc. Behav.* 19:15.
26. MARMOT, M. G. et al. (1975) 'Epidemiologic studies of coronary heart disease and stroke in Japanese men living in Japan, Hawaii, and California'. *Am. J. Epidemiol.* 102, 6: 514.
27. HAYNES, S. G., EAKER, E. D. and FEINLEIB, M. (1983) Spouse behavior and coronary heart disease in men: Prospective results from the Framingham heart study, *Am. J. Epidemiol.* 118: 1.
28. SOSA, R. et al. (1980) 'The effect of a supportive

companion in perinatal problems, length of labour and mother–infant interaction'. *New Eng. J. Med.* 303: 597.
29. KLAUS, M. H. et al (1986) 'Effects of social support during parturition on maternal and infant morbidity'. *BMJ* 293: 585.
30. HAYNES, S. G., FEINLEIB, M. and KANNEL, W. B. (1980) 'The relationship of psychosocial factors to coronary heart disease in The Framingham Study 111. Eight year incidence of coronary heart disease'. *Am. J. Epidemiol.* 111: 37.

6
FITNESS

```
STRESSOR → STRESS (Stress Reaction) → STRAIN (Effects of Stress)

SUPPORT        SELF (The Individual)
```

We turn now to the characteristics which may make us, as individuals, more resistant to the effects of stress. The first is fitness.

The fit individual is far less likely to suffer from the effects of stress than the unfit.[1] It is important, therefore, that we become and stay as fit as possible. So how do we get fit and keep fit? Modern preventive medicine knows a good deal about keeping fit and healthy.

Exercise

Exercise, such as walking briskly, jogging, running, skipping and swimming, has been shown in many studies to be good for us, both physically and mentally:

- it is good for our heart, lungs and arteries and protects us from premature heart disease;
- it is good for our bowels, and keeps us regular;
- it tones up muscles and so protects our backs, joints and ligaments;
- it is good for our bones, because inactivity allows our bones to thin and makes them liable to fracture, (astronauts in a weightless environment lose bone very quickly and are now instructed to exercise regularly);
- it makes us feel good;
- it gives us a better self image;
- it is one of the best tranquillisers that we can get;
- it helps us sleep;
- it is good for depression;
- it makes us more alert and more responsive;
- it is good for our sex life;
- it releases chemicals which can counteract pain—our own individual pain killers, endorphins and encaphalins;
- it keeps our weight down, and gives us a better figure.

So it is important to get enough exercise of the right type. The type, duration and severity of the exercise advisable depends on a number of factors (sex, age, general health, etc) and a personal programme especially designed for the individual is ideal. In our longer seminars, we can use a computerised system to assess fitness and then provide an individual exercise programme. It is impossible to do this here but we can lay down a number of general principles.

Guidelines

Before starting exercise, obtain medical advice if you are seeing a doctor regularly or taking medication for any complaint. If you are over the age of forty-five, you should in any case have a general health check-up before beginning an exercise programme.

Start slowly and steadily and exercise regularly.

The exercise should make you slightly out of breath, but you should still be able to talk while exercising. 'Walk at a talking pace'. If you are too puffed to talk then you are overdoing it. If you do not get out of breath at all, it is not doing you much good.

If you have not been taking much exercise, then start with five to ten minutes walking, three or four times a week. Gradually increase this by about five minutes a week and also gradually increase the pace, eventually including some hills if necessary. You will find that you can gradually increase the distance without getting more out of breath.

Over a period of several months, gradually increase the exercise to about thirty to forty minutes, three or four times per week.

If you are young and already reasonably fit you can break into a jog without getting too much out of breath and eventually you may be able to jog for the whole thirty to forty minutes.

If you get any symptoms at all when exercising, especially such as pains in the chest or legs or feeling faint, then stop the exercise immediately. *Never* try to exercise through it, and always consult your doctor.

Wear comfortable and sensible clothing and comfortable and supportive footwear.

Be careful of uneven ground.

Walking or jogging outside, especially in winter and in the dark, can be difficult; the same effects can be achieved by walking or running on the spot indoors or in the carport or in the garage, as long as the door is left open to let any lingering car fumes out. If fit, you can progress to skipping. Swimming is equally good, and may be easier and better for those with arthritis of the knees, hips or ankles. For some, cycling may be easier and an indoor exercise cycle can be a boon.

Even the old and infirm benefit from exercise and the same general principles apply about getting a little out of breath, etc. If you are completely immobile and cannot run, jog, swim, cycle or jog, then exercise of the arms may be possible and can have benefits.

If you are keen on sport, then golf, tennis, football, etc., can add to the enjoyment of exercise, but it must be regular (three or four times a week for at least thirty to forty minutes) and you should be slightly out of breath while taking part in the sport. Of course, your one round of golf at the weekend can be augmented by walking, jogging, etc, during the week.

Weight watching

Being overweight makes you more liable to suffer from a whole number of conditions, like high blood pressure, heart disease, gall bladder disease, arthritis, bad back, diabetes and varicose veins. On the other hand, being within normal limits makes you feel fitter physically and mentally, gives you a better self image and makes you better able to withstand stressors.

I am often asked what one's ideal weight would be. There are very sophisticated ways of calculating this but there are also quite simple ones. Charts showing the desirable range of weight for each person's height are available. We always get some comedian who says, 'I am not really overweight. What is wrong is that I am not tall enough. I was really meant to be taller—look at my short legs.'

Unfortunately, there is little you can do about your height so the only answer is to deal with your weight. Apart from the height/weight charts, if you are honest with yourself you know when you are overweight or are putting on weight: your trousers, skirts, dresses, shirts are all getting tight (and not by being shrunk in the wash) and you begin to need bigger sizes. One good test is to strip off and stand in front of a full length mirror (often not a pretty sight!) so you can judge honestly if you are too fat. If you jump up and down and everything wobbles, you are definitely overweight!

Guidelines

What do you do to lose weight or ensure that you keep within the normal range? We have already dealt with regular exercise (and this can help) but the main way is to control what you eat. It is good to have an individual programme but this is not essential, and we can cover only the general points here. Crash diets, unless you are grossly overweight and this is already affecting your health, are out. Ordinary or sensible reducing diets—there are many available—are enough, but these can be boring and irksome.

In general terms, if you have a reasonably balanced diet, all you have to do is eat less of everything. In fact, having a *strategy* is more important than actually having a diet. Planning to avoid temptation is an immense help! Avoid a seat near the buffet car when travelling by train, or choose a train with no buffet. Visit the grocers or supermarket after a meal, not when hungry. Have a list of what is needed before going, and stick to it. Of course, the supermarket wants to sell more and loves it when you walk round seeing things that you think you need. You should not buy unnecessary food or keep it in the house, then it is not handy or a temptation. It is better not to have snacks in the house so that you cannot eat snacks between meals. Buy smaller plates! Psychologically you feel cheated if your plate is not full. Dish out a little less of everything.

The aim is to lose a little weight slowly; there is less likelihood of putting weight back on quickly if it is lost slowly with good strategies. Many people have found attendance at Weight Watchers' classes useful and a spur to losing weight, although classes do not suit everyone.

Hints on a healthy diet

Apart from the amount you eat, it is also important that you eat a balanced, healthy diet.

On the whole, 'fad' foods are not necessary and can be expensive. There are some people who are genuinely allergic to some foods and to dyes and preservatives, and there are some who need extra iron or vitamins or minerals, but they are few in number; for the majority, mainstream medical opinion is now fairly well agreed about what is good and what is not. It is a myth that whatever is 'natural' must be good for us: there are many natural plants which are poisonous and many naturally occurring minerals and substances are toxic. We know the risk of drinking natural untreated milk and so have accepted that pasteurised milk is safer.

Avoid all sweet things—sugar, sweets, cakes, biscuits. They provide 'empty' calories: very little nutrition, but help to put on weight.

Also, fatty greasy foods are not good for you—sausages, fat meat, hamburgers, roast potatoes, chips, fries. Instead, eat lean meat, fish, chicken and grilled rather than fried foods. It is only in recent years that the harm animal fat can bring to your arteries and heart has been realised.

Because of their high cholesterol content and potential harm to arteries and heart, dairy products should also be eaten in moderation only—butter, cheese, cream, full cream milk, eggs. Cottage cheese and skimmed or half cream milk is better for you, and low fat margarine is better than butter.

Extra salt can be bad for some people with a tendency to high blood pressure, and it is best to use only a modicum in cooking, and not to add more at the table. At one establishment during a Healthy Eating Week, we agreed with the catering staff that no salt would be added to food during cooking. None of the customers noticed or complained. However, they still all added their own salt.

The best diet includes fish, chicken, lean meat, vegetables (including potatoes, especially baked in their jackets), and salads, fruit, bread (especially brown wholemeal bread with low fat margarine), and cereals, particularly oatmeal. As a Scotsman, I was delighted to learn that porridge was good for my health!

Check-ups

Regular check-ups can detect certain conditions in their early stages, and early treatment can prevent severe consequences later.

Regular blood pressure checks are very important, especially after the age of forty. Measurement is the only way of telling if your blood pressure is raised, and getting and keeping it under control is usually quite easy and can prevent strokes and heart attacks.

In women, cervical smears can detect the precancerous stage of cancer of the cervix; some authorities advise it every three to five years in women between twenty and sixty-five years of age. Mammograms (breast screening) can detect cancer of the breast before it can otherwise be found, thus allowing very early treatment. Some authorities advise this in women aged fifty to sixty-four every three years.

Measurement of blood cholesterol is recommended for those who are at special risk of developing coronary artery disease, although not all authorities agree that it should be carried out routinely.

Summary

The fit individual is less likely to suffer from the effects of stress, so get and stay fit.

1. Get sufficient exercise. If possible, get an individual programme from an expert. Start slowly, work up to thirty to forty minutes, three or four times a week, and always get a little out of breath. If ill, on medicines, or in any doubt about your fitness to start, consult your own doctor.
2. Watch your weight; exercise; eat less; have a 'strategy'.
3. Eat a balanced diet. Fads are usually not necessary. Avoid all sweet things and all fatty or greasy foods. Cut down on dairy foods and salt. Eat plenty of fish, chicken, lean meat, vegetables, fruit and cereals.
4. Check-ups, especially routine blood pressure checks, are recommended.

Note

1. JACOB, R. G. and CHESNEY, M. A. (1986) 'Psychological and behavioral methods to reduce cardiovascular reactivity' in *Handbook of Stress, reactivity, and cardiovascular disease*. K. A. Matthews, S. M. Weiss, T. Detre, T. M. Dembrowski, B. F. Falkner, S. B. Manuck and R. B. Williams Jr. (eds) Wiley, New York.

7
A HEALTHY LIFESTYLE

Those with a healthy lifestyle are less likely to feel pressures and to suffer from the effects of stress.

The age of rush

This is the age of rush. In 1967, testimony before a US Senate sub-committee indicated that by 1985 people could be working just twenty-two hours per week, or twenty-seven weeks a year, or could retire by the age of thirty-eight. In the UK, it seems only a few years ago that there was concern at the prospect of so much leisure; a start was proposed to educate people to use their leisure and plans were made to provide facilities. Yet now time is at a premium, and for many people their day is so filled that they have no time to relax.

In New York (and what happens in the USA often follows in the UK and Europe) yuppies nowadays order gourmet takeaway food rather than microwave dinners as these are too much trouble.

Canary sales are up—low maintenance pets.

Beaujolais nouveau sales are booming—a wine one need not wait for!

Parents have so little time for their children that they have to leave cards on the breakfast table ('Have a good day at school') or under the pillow at night ('Wish I were here to tuck you in').

What has happened to all this talk of more leisure time? Many people are working longer hours, and the underlying reason seems to be the need for affluence, more money and a higher standard of living.

There is a big temptation, for businessmen to take so much work home that they never have any days in the week off work at all. Workers apparently need to bring in more money, so they do overtime at weekends or moonlight (take another job) so that they also never have a full day off. The problem nowadays is that many people think they will not get through their work, or have enough money coming in, if they do not work seven days a week.

To free more capital, people sell their houses and move further and further from their workplaces in the cities to cheaper housing areas. This means commuting to work, so many hours are added to their travel time and thus to the working week.

When I worked in the pharmaceutical industry I worked very long hours. I often had to travel to the USA or around Europe at weekends to get to meetings on Monday mornings; when I did have weekends at home, I spent the whole time reading to keep up with the increasing amount of research worldwide. This was a typical work pattern in that industry.

Rest and relaxation

Batteries which are run and run eventually become weaker and give out. The same thing will happen to your body and brain if they are not given the opportunity, through rest, relaxation and sleep, to be recharged.

It is important that you try as far as possible to take one day in seven completely free of work. Remember, seven days make one weak! Various ratios of rest days have been tried to see which are most efficient. One day in ten has been tried in some countries but has not caught on. The best still seems to be one in seven.

Go on holiday regularly, despite the fear that there will be an accumulation of work when you return because no one is available to cover when you are away. You will be better able to deal with everything when you return. The holiday should be long enough to give you time to wind down and then enjoy the period of relaxation. Some people wind down more slowly than others, so each holiday period needed varies from individual to individual. The holiday too should be restful, not packed with activities, especially stressful ones like exciting pastimes or hours and hours of driving, travelling and visiting.

Get enough sleep. The exact amount required by individuals varies a good deal; older people tend to need less than younger, but somewhere around eight hours per night should be the norm. It is not known exactly why we need to sleep rather than just rest, but one current theory is that sleep allows the brain, unoccupied with any other thoughts, time to resort and refile misfiled information—a process we become aware of in dreaming.

Restful sleep is essential. Give yourself the chance of getting good sleep. Sleeping pills should really be an absolutely last resort, as they interfere with dreaming. A cup of warm milk (containing chemicals which help sleep) combined with a restful pastime is a good idea before retiring. (A television horror or drama late at night is not the best recipe for restful sleep!) There are a number of techniques for assisting sleep and we teach individuals what we believe is best suited to them.

Find a way of relaxing which suits you. For centuries it has been known that listening to good music, singing, playing an instrument, reading good books, reading or writing poetry, admiring and enjoying good art or spending time painting or drawing are relaxing pastimes. Many great men and women carrying heavy political or social burdens have found peace and refreshment in these pursuits. Winston Churchill had his painting, Edward Heath his music. When did you last engage in any of them?

Avoid obsession!

If we are going to relax properly then it follows that we cannot be for ever occupied with work and what has to be done. Yet so often we pack every available hour and day and page in our diaries with some activity that we have been asked to do, or feel that we should do, or feel that no one else can do as well as we can. This is a mistake. We must have time to relax and we must have time for ourselves. Someone has suggested that we actually make a date with ourselves in our diaries so that when requests and possibilities come we can honestly say, 'Sorry. I have an appointment on that day at that time and only I can attend.' It is much easier to do this than to make excuses, or even to explain 'I have blocked this time out to relax.'

A few years ago, I was asked to see a director of one of the country's biggest public companies. I was told that the chairman was concerned about him because he was not performing as well as he had and could. He was forgetting things, did not seem to concentrate well at meetings and was being difficult with colleagues and short with his secretary. It seemed obvious from what I had been told that this director was suffering from the effects of stress. My mind ran on as I prepared to see him. Doubtless he was a workaholic, doing far too much and never relaxing. Advice about relaxation and taking up a hobby would be good, sensible advice.

When we met, I did establish quite quickly that this man had a very stressful job, was working very long hours and usually had to take work home. He confirmed that he was not performing well and wondered whether he had some medical condition. Thorough clinical examination confirmed that apart from slightly raised blood pressure there was nothing abnormal to be found. My diagnosis was therefore 'effects of stress'.

'I think you should seriously consider relaxing more. Why not take up a hobby?' I asked.

'I do have a hobby, gardening. I spend as much time as I can at weekends in the garden.'

So much for my first line of advice! Gardening should be relaxing and should also be providing our director with exercise—depending, of course, on the type of gardening.

'What type of gardening do you like?' I asked.

'Oh, everything,' he replied, and with that he produced from his pocket several sheets of paper. 'Here are my tasks for this weekend. Thirteen on Saturday and twelve on Sunday. See, I have them all detailed and timed.'

So much for a relaxing hobby, I thought. Our director was as ordered, obsessive and perfectionist about his gardening, his hobby, as he was about his work. Granted, it was a change at the weekend and gardening can be relaxing and good exercise, but this was not. He was exchanging his weekly work for his weekend work.

It is important that we have a relaxing hobby that absorbs us without its becoming another stressor.

Use time efficiently

We are all given the same days in a week, hours in a day, minutes in an hour. When one day is ended, we cannot bank any of the minutes or hours for another time. They must be used by the end of the day. It is important, therefore, that we use them to best advantage if we are to get through the work and the tasks which have to be done, and not feel under constant pressure.

A useful memorandum for using your time better is the 'Three D' rule:

Discontinue low priority activities altogether, to give time for the more important. Most people spend 80% of their time on the least important issues.

Delegate. I realise that some people have no one to delegate to, but many have. Do you always delegate when you can? It is good practice wherever possible only to do what only you can do, and delegate the rest. But you must be honest and fair about what really is essential for you to do. So often we do something because we think no one will do it as well. Maybe this does not always matter, especially if it frees us to concentrate on the really important things that only we can do.

Do things more efficiently. This you must learn and apply. Time and motion studies, better organisational files, use of computer, word processors and other time saving devices are worth considering. Many good books are available on this subject (eg *Seconds Away* by Dr David Cormack).[1]

Planning priorities

While it is good to learn from the past and plan for the future, it is pointless to worry about what has been or about what is to come, as neither can be affected now. Better to concentrate on the task in hand and what is happening now. It pays to spend some time on planning and getting short term priorities right. Do not get bogged down with the urgent to the exclusion of the important as so many do. You can do only one thing at a time. Unless trained to, your brain cannot cope with two similar types of task at the same time and you will end up doing neither well.

Learn to differentiate between tasks which are urgent and those which are important. It is good advice to:

do what is important *and* urgent;

delegate (if you can) what is urgent but not important;

draw up plans for what is important but not urgent;

drop what is neither urgent nor important.

So the first task is to assess your major priorities. History shows that many men and women do not give the time and weight and interest and priority to those things in life which they believe are the most important to them, often with resulting strain and disastrous consequences.

What or who are the most important things in life to you? Do you always act as if they are?

Put a number from 1 to 8 on the *right* of each of the following items, in the order that you think they should be given priority in your life.

Work	Religious/church activities	Your children
Your spouse	Your family/parents etc	God
'Good works'	Personal interests	

Now go back and put a number on the *left* of the above in the order that you are *actually* giving them priority in your life. If the numbers on the right and left are not the same, what do you intend to do?

Is your job more important to you than your wife or husband, or your children? If it is not, then why do you put it before them, at the risk of losing them either physically or emotionally? Are your parents more important to you in the end than your wife or husband or children? If not, why do you seem often to put their claims on you before those of your husband, wife or children?

It is important that you actually decide who and what are the most important people in your life. It is important that you do put them first when it comes to allocating attention, time and resources.

Unfortunately, and often tragically, no conscious decision is made about our main life priorities. We have never thought it through. Is it surprising then that we may get it wrong when it comes to how we think and behave? Frequently we hear of people who are successful in their fields—business, music, acting, sport, etc—whose homes and family lives are in ruins. Did they actually decide that their job and career were more important than their family? Yet they have spent most of their time in the office, travelling, away from home as their spouse and children grew further apart and pressures on the family and home grew.

It is tragic that they may only become aware of where their priorities actually lie when it is too late, a wife becomes depressed, a husband walks out or children get into trouble. These tragedies, of course, are not confined to the rich and famous, but can affect any family where priorities have not been properly set.

Summary

1. Get adequate rest, relaxation and sleep. Take at least one day off in seven. Take long enough holidays to allow a period of wind down.
2. Do not overwork or take on too much. Learn to say 'No' sometimes. Make regular dates with yourself.
3. Spend time listening to music, singing, playing an instrument, or reading good books, reading or writing poetry, admiring great art or beauty.
4. Use time efficiently.
5. Live one day at a time.
6. Plan time.
7. Get your priorities right.

Note

1. CORMACK, D. (1986) *Seconds Away*. MARC Europe.

Further reading

Seconds Away. David Cormack, MARC Europe, 1986.
Managing Your Time. T. W. Engstrom and R. A. Mackenzie. Zondervan, 1967.

8
YOUR SELF IMAGE

People who believe in themselves and are committed to what they are doing do not feel threatened by events in their lives; they deal with the world in a relaxed fashion, and they deal well with stressors.[1-4]

However, if you lack this confidence, or if you have an inferiority complex, you may find stressors too much for you and suffer from the effects of stress.

It is important, therefore, that you have a good self image and a high esteem of yourself, that you think you are worth something, count for something, mean something, and that what you are doing is worthwhile. Unfortunately, many people have a very poor self image. They apologise for everything that happens and almost apologise for being alive. There are others who appear confident on the surface but when you really get to know them, or if they let the façade fall, you find that they think very little of themselves. They are often riddled by self doubt.

How do you maintain a good self image? If it is poor, can it be changed, and if so, how?

Poor self image

First, if you do have a poor self image you must understand why this is and how this affects you and your ability to cope with stressors.

From an early age it becomes very clear to us that to be worthwhile, to be thought well of, or to count for something, we must achieve.

It seems that your parents praise you, reward you and think more of you and love you more if you do well; they are annoyed and tell you off and do not love you when you do not do well. This idea is reinforced at school. You are more important and more notice is taken of you if you do well and achieve high marks in examinations; teachers make a point of telling you either that you have done well, or that you are not very clever. In sport, you become popular and are thought much of if you win, if you play for the first eleven or the first fifteen, and even more so if you achieve enough to represent your school, your district, your county or country.

Every part of modern culture—society, the media, your friends—all tell you that you are worthwhile if you achieve status, money, a good marriage, and 2.4 children. And so all the way through life your image seems to depend on what you achieve, at home, at school, at sport, in work, in life.[10]

If you do well in many of these things, or even in some or one of them, then you feel good about yourself. And if you feel good about yourself, you have a good self image, and then you can cope well with stressors.

If, however, you do not do well, then you feel that you have failed. To begin with you may try again. You may try harder at something, with increasing tension and anxiety, but if you continue to fail at different times and in different areas of your life, you become disillusioned and frustrated. Then either you get angry and resentful with life in general and begin to rebel, or you get angry with yourself and feel depressed. In time, you think not only that you have failed, but that you are a failure. Once you think that you are not really very good, and eventually pretty worthless, useless and inadequate, then you stop trying altogether and withdraw from the outside world. You feel rejected and lonely.

In other words, a poor self image is often the result of your reaction over the years to your apparent inability to achieve, and your reaction to what others say to you about this. Your self image eventually reaches rock bottom and, when stressors come along, you know that you cannot cope. That is when you begin to suffer from the effects of stress.

Some well-meaning friends will tell you from time to time that you are not really as useless as you have come to believe and you need not feel bad about things. You find it hard to believe them because failure, and the fear of failure, continues.

Things may get to the point where you consult or are sent to a psychologist or counsellor. They will help to show you that you are not all bad, that you have rights— including the right to be wrong, to fail and to assert yourself. You may be helped to some extent, but unfortunately, often what you believe the rest of the world thinks of you is reality to you: the feelings of inadequacy and poor self image continue, and the effects of stress become obvious when you have to contend with stressors.

Believe in yourself

It is very important indeed to come to believe that your worth is *not* in what you have achieved, but in who you are. After all, do you love your children less when they fail? Do you love your wife less when she burns the roast? Do you love your husband less when he does not get promotion at work? The answer, I suspect, in each case is 'no'.

It is important that we affirm each other—that husbands tell their wives how wonderful they are and vice versa. It is important that we tell our children that we love them and think they are wonderful at all times, not just when they succeed.

It is important also to be committed to what you are doing in life, whatever that is—a captain of industry, a postman, mother or father, a student, an old age pensioner, or unemployed. Sometimes it is difficult to feel that your role is important and to feel particularly committed to it. Some people take up a cause, often all-consuming and often very laudable—a political party, anti-racism, human rights, anti-vivisection, or 'greenery'. Anything which arouses your enthusiasm and gives you tasks to which you feel committed will help you to feel useful and important, and help your self image.

Crucial needs

You have been created with two deep inner needs: for love and security; and for significance or meaning and purpose in life.[5]

Along with all mankind you have believed (whether you have consciously been aware of it or not) that you can totally meet these needs in a variety of ways—by your love and security from spouse, family, children, friends, savings, insurance, the state, the NHS, and by being in control of your life at all times. Your significance, you believe, can be met from your job, your status, position, authority, knowledge, degrees, possessions, spouse or partner, affairs or your looks.[6]

As long as your needs for love and security and significance continue to be met from any of these sources, you feel good, happy, at peace with the world and have a good self image; your emotions and your life are stable; there is no threat to you. But if your love and security or significance is lost because one of the sources you have been depending on is taken away, or even if there is a threat of it being taken away, then you can very soon begin to suffer from the effects of stress, with a lowering of self esteem.[7-9]

It may have happened to you or to someone you know: people who have 'gone to pieces' and developed the effects of stress when faced with a spouse rejecting them for someone else, or the death of a spouse or child; redundancy or threat of redundancy; demotion; stock market crash; business crash; serious illness; and so on.

It is important that you review your life periodically and ask yourself 'Where am I getting my love and security and my significance? Can I utterly rely on these sources, and if not, what can I do to ensure against losing them?' When you feel safe and secure that your fundamental needs will be met, you feel confident to face the world, and so you deal well with any stress.

Summary

1. People who believe in themselves are less likely to suffer the effects of stress.
2. It is important to have a good self image and to be committed to what you are doing.
3. Self image need not depend on achievement.
4. Your crucial needs are for love and security, significance, worth and value. Try to ensure dependable sources for these.

Notes

1. PAULHUS, D. and CHRISTIE, R. (1981) 'Spheres of control: An interactionist approach to assessment of perceived control' in *Research with the locus of control construct.* H. M. Lefcourt (ed.), Academic Press, New York.
2. GOTTLIEB, B. H. (ed.) (1983) *Social Support Strategies.* Sage, Beverley Hills, C.A.
3. WILLS, T. A. (1985) 'Supportive functions of interpersonal

relations' in *Social Support and Health*. S. Cohen and L. Syme (eds), Academic Press, New York.
4. KOBASA, S. (1979) 'Stressful life events, personality, health. An enquiry into hardiness'. *J. Pers. & Soc. Psychol.* 37.
5. MASLOW, A. H. (1954) *Motivation and Personality*. 2nd edition, Harper & Row, New York.
6. IVANCEVICH, J. M. and MATTESON, M. T. (1988) 'Type A behavior and the healthy individual'. *Br. J. Med. Psychol.* 61: 37.
7. LAZARUS, R. S. (1966) *Psychological Stress and the Coping Process*. McGraw-Hill, New York.
8. HOUSE, J. S. (1981) *Work Stress and Social Support*. Addison-Wesley, Reading, M. A.
9. COHEN, S., EVANS, G. W., STOKOLS, D. and KRANTZ, D. S. (1986) *Behavior, Health and Environmental Stress*. Plenum, New York.
10. IVANCEVICH, J. M. and MATTESON, M. T. (1988) 'Type A behavior and the healthy individual'. *Br. J. Med. Psychol.* 61: 37.

9
ATTITUDES TO LIFE

Different people react differently to stressors. For general purposes we can divide them into two groups, 'Type A' and 'Type B'. Each group tends to have certain common characteristics in various areas of life, as well as in response to stress.[1-14]

Type A

A typical Type A is often slim, very ambitious, fiercely competitive, always active, busy and in a hurry; he talks fast, often interrupts, and finishes other people's sentences for them. He is often a workaholic and burns the candle at both ends; even his relaxations and hobbies are active and often exciting—hang-gliding, driving fast cars, scuba diving. He may be quite aggressive to get where and what he wants; he is impatient and quite often shows this and his hostility; he is sometimes known as the AHA personality—Angry, Hostile, Aggressive;[15] he welcomes change and thrives on it and on pressure. However, he does react strongly to stressors, especially if he is aggressive and hostile. His way of life may take its toll and he may well, after too much pressure, develop high blood pressure and suffer a heart attack or a stroke.[16-23]

If you think you are a Type A person, it is important

that you make an effort to change your behaviour if such consequences are to be avoided.[24-30]

Hints for type As

Review the stressors in your life and discard or alter the ones you are inflicting on yourself because of your Type A personality: the punishing schedule, the over-numerous responsibilities, possibly even the consuming ambitions.

Do not take on more than you can handle. It is better not to take something on than to make a mess of it. You may let someone down if you do not manage to come up with the goods, or if you become ill and therefore fail to fulfill any of your obligations.

Your lifestyle must change. Make time for relaxing holidays and hobbies. Try to slow down and not put yourself under constant time pressures. Leave more time to accomplish things. Leave for the airport or train or appointment earlier so that you are not always in a rush. Talk, walk and drive more slowly. When you find yourself speeding up, tell yourself to slow down. Listen more, talk and interrupt less.

Let the train take the strain instead of driving fast everywhere. Driving is a very big stressor. London taxi drivers suffer a high incidence of coronary artery disease —partly, possibly, because of smoking, lack of exercise, and exposure to petrol and diesel fumes, but also, possibly, from the pressure of driving itself.

Do one thing at a time. Put other things out of your mind and concentrate on the task in hand. Accept what you cannot change. Smile, even when you don't feel like it—it relaxes you.

Enjoy delays. You might as well, since the chances are that you can do nothing about the traffic jam, striking air traffic controllers, British Rail staff shortages, or late delivery of supplies. Read, listen to music, enjoy the scenery, and switch off.

Make a real effort to stop smoking: different techniques like special chewing gum and self-help 'Stop' groups are available. Make sure your alcohol consumption stays at a healthy level. For a man, this should probably be no more than twenty-one units per week, and for a woman probably not more than fourteen per week (one unit = 1 pint beer, 1 small short of spirits, 1 sherry, or 1 glass of wine).

A number of techniques are available to help you relax and some also appear to begin to change your attitude to life and relaxation. Simple or progressive relaxation exercises are easy to learn. You are taught to tense certain groups of muscles and then allow them to relax, paying attention to your breathing.[31] Biofeedback is also helpful when you first try relaxation. You are attached to a sound or light 'relaxometer', which indicates when you are relaxed or tense—from this you can learn how to relax.[32]

The Alexander technique concentrates on relaxation through correct posture and some find this helpful.[33] We have already referred to music as a means of relaxing, and some people have taken this further and offer music therapy for relaxation.[34] Massage, either from a qualified teacher, or simple stroking from spouse or friend, can also be very relaxing. Training in basic autogenic exercises is possibly the most powerful technique of all.[35]

All these techniques should be learned from a qualified and responsible teacher, and ideally under medical supervision. Techniques involving Eastern religions and philosophies and the occult are best avoided.

Be willing to change

While some of these techniques can produce relaxation and *may* lead to a change in Type A behaviour, it is important that you not only practice relaxation techniques but also put the hints for Type As into practice. Unfortunately, as a Type A individual you may find it difficult to change or even to want to change your behaviour; it may take the shock of your first heart attack—if you survive—to bring home to you the need for a changed life.

In counselling situations we are often asked what behaviour a Type A should change. Our usual reply is to ask the individual what he would change after his first heart attack, and then to urge him to consider which of these changes it would be sensible to consider now. We have been impressed by how much Type A individuals know about how they are stressing themselves and what needs to be changed. However, we have also been impressed by how little and how seldom the Type A is willing or able to change his behaviour. He is often addicted to it and enjoys it. But even if he wants to, he finds it difficult to relax and slow down.

Recently, John developed pains across his chest and went to see his GP. The diagnosis was angina and high blood pressure, and he was prescribed pills for his high blood pressure and for his heart. He was also put on a diet as his blood fats were high. The specialist did say that since he did not smoke, was not overweight, and his father, uncles and brothers were all alive and well with no trouble from their hearts (all well-known risk factors for heart problems) that his problem might be associated with stress. It was at this point that John was persuaded by his wife to see me.

John was in his early forties. He was a manager in a medium-sized company, he was ambitious, he wanted to get to the top and he had been working very long hours recently.

He travelled a good deal all over the UK in his company car visiting suppliers, as he thought this was better than phone calls or letters, and was the best way of ensuring that he got exactly what he wanted. Although his assistant managers could go, this was too important to leave to them, so he usually went himself. He also had to fly fairly frequently in Europe.

Recently he had been drinking more, especially at nights as he was not sleeping too well. He was not overweight for his height. His fingers were not nicotine-stained. His blood pressure, now under the influence of the pills, was a little on the high side. His heart sounded healthy. I noticed that he bit his nails.

John wanted to know what I could do for him and how quickly. I explained that stress was almost certainly associated with his condition. He was a typical Type A, and I advised that he slow down and change his behaviour. I recommended a course of relaxation exercises (see p. 66) and advised that in parallel with this we should have some sessions to help him change his Type A behaviour and his attitudes to work and living.

John did, indeed, start the course, but found that he could not spare the five minutes or so three times a day to do the exercises. After two weeks he gave up with profuse apologies. He said he would try to slow down but neither I, nor his wife, nor John himself believed that he would.

Not unexpectedly, things got worse, and John was admitted to an intensive care unit with a moderately severe heart attack. Eventually, he needed a heart by-pass operation. He has recovered well from that and is now back at work. I do hope he now decides to change his Type A behaviour either before he has another heart attack, which could kill him, or needs another bypass.

While observing the hints for Type As and practising one of the relaxation techniques can lead to a change in Type A behaviour, a basic change in attitude to living may be needed.

Type B

A typical Type B, on the other hand, is often well built, phlegmatic, laid back, and takes things as they come. Type B does not get worked up about things, he is not very ambitious, not aggressive and is slower in all he does than Type A. He is less likely to suffer from blood pressure and heart disease, but if he puts on too much weight then these conditions and others can also be brought on.

Although there are very typical Type As and Type Bs, many people are a combination of both, with a tendency to one type or the other.

The power of emotions

Faced with stressors, some forms of cancer and other conditions may be more likely to develop in those who bottle up emotions, who often feel hopeless and helpless.[36-37] When expression of emotion is encouraged, cancer seems less likely to develop.[38] So let your emotions come out. Do not be afraid to cry even if you are a man. Do not be afraid to laugh and smile. Look on the bright side of things. Talk in an optimistic way. Try to mix with people who are strong and optimistic rather than those who spread gloom and doom.

People who harbour resentment or bitterness over things that have happened to them may, when exposed to stressors, be more likely to develop chronic diseases like some forms of rheumatoid arthritis. I have seen many people with rheumatoid arthritis, and indeed other chronic conditions, where something has happened in the past which still rankles. Often they say: 'I will never forgive—for walking out on me/for passing me over for promotion/for what they did to my family' and so on. Unfortunately for them, the only harm they are doing through their bitterness is to themselves and their own health. Often the object of their bitterness is no longer bothered by the past situation or is even aware that bitterness is still harboured. It is important, therefore, that you forgive and forget, and if possible make up.

The lonely can suffer from changes in immunity and may develop the effects of stress.[39] Separated or divorced persons with subsequent loneliness are more likely to have psychiatric problems than married people,[40] more often to suffer from alcohol problems, depression and suicides.[41] Studies have shown that the separated and divorced suffer more acute and chronic illnesses[42] and visit doctors 30% more frequently than do the married or single.[43] They also have a higher mortality rate from things like pneumonia, TB, heart disease and some types of cancer.

The bereaved, again suffering from loneliness, show lower immunity[44] and are at risk from certain diseases and have higher mortality rates.[45]

Unfortunately, the divorce rate in the UK in 1987, which stood at 12.6 per thousand marriages, is exceeded only by Denmark with 12.7. Also the number of one-person households in Great Britain has increased from 12% of households in 1961 to 26% in 1988 (Germany is even higher at 31% followed by Denmark at 29%).[46] A recent editorial about social trends in *Public Health* states

> the large number of small families is one of the major problems which we will have to face in the future, including

as it does the large number of old people living alone, as well as an increasing number of one-parent families. Since man is a social animal, needing the support of family and friends, we can expect an increase in social and mental problems from this fact alone.[47]

It is important, therefore, that you avoid loneliness as far as possible. Try not to hide yourself away. If you find it difficult to find company and friendship elsewhere, have you thought of looking for it in a friendly and caring church?

People who have deep, hidden emotions—hidden in the subconscious—like anger, grief, disappointment, and frustration, may be more vulnerable to stressors and liable to suffer from anxiety, phobias or psychosomatic effects of stress, like migraine, dysmennorrhea, asthma and the like. It is important that hidden emotions are uncovered. It may be necessary to get help from a counsellor to uncover them so that they can be dealt with.

Share your problems

People who can open up about their problems rather than keeping them to themselves are likely to be less vulnerable to stressors.

In a recent study,[48] fifty students were randomly allocated to two groups. One group of twenty-five were asked to write for twenty minutes a day for four days on events they had found difficult or stressful or had hurt them. The other control group of students were asked to write about unimportant, trivial subjects, like the shoes they were wearing.

Following the writing exercise, immunity of all the students was measured. Interestingly, the group who had written about the stressful things that had happened to them showed increased immunity. The health of this group also seemed to be better than the health of those who had written about trivial things, as they visited the health centre on fewer occasions following the writing exercise. In this group, the biggest immunity changes of all were in those who wrote about things that they had never told anyone about before.

It is wise, therefore, not to bottle up problems but to find someone, spouse, close friend, or trained counsellor with whom you can be absolutely open and to confide your problems and fears to them.

Summary

1. Type A individuals, especially the angry, hostile and aggressive, are more likely to suffer from high blood pressure, heart attacks and strokes.
2. Relaxation techniques can help to change behaviour.
3. It is important to change your whole attitude to life.
4. To avoid certain other effects of stress:
    forgive and forget,
    do not bottle up your emotions,
    try to be optimistic,
    avoid loneliness,
    uncover and deal with hidden emotions,
    share your problems.

Notes

1. EYSENCK, H. J. (1967) *The Biological Basis of Personality*. Thomas, Springfield, I.L.
2. ROSENMAN, R. H., BRAND, R. J., JENKINS, C. D. et al. (1975) 'Coronary heart disease in the Western Collaborative Group Study: Final follow-up experience of $8\frac{1}{2}$ years'. *JAMA.*, 233: 872.
3. ROSKIES, E. (1983) 'Stress management for Type A individuals' in *Stress Reduction and Prevention*. D. Melchenbaum and M. Jaremko (eds), New York.

4. HAYNES, S. G., FEINLEIB, M. and KANNEL, W. B., (1980) 'The relationship of psychosocial factors to coronary heart disease in The Framingham Study 111. Eight year incidence of coronary heart disease'. *Am. J. Epidemiol.* 111: 37.
5. REVIEW PANEL (1981) 'Coronary-prone behavior and coronary heart disease: A critical review'. *Circulation* 63: 1199.
6. COOPER, T., DETRE, T. and WEISS, S. M. (1981) 'Coronary prone behavior and coronary heart disease: A critical review'. *Circulation* 63: 1199.
7. PRICE, V. A. (1982) *Type A Behavior Pattern*. Academic Press, New York. See also RAHE, R. H. (1968) 'Life-change measurement as a predictor of illness' *Proc. Roy. Soc. Med.* 61: 1124.
8. ROSKIES, E. (1983) 'Stress management for Type A individuals' in *Stress Reduction and Prevention*. D. Melchenbaum and M. Jaremko (eds), New York.
9. EYSENCK, H. J. (1985(a)) 'Personality, cancer and cardiovascular disease: a causal analysis, in *Personality and Individual Differences*, 5: 535.
10. EYSENCK, H. J. and EYSENCK, M. W. (1985(b)) *Personality and Individual Differences*. Plenum Press, New York.
11. WRIGHT, R. A., CONTRADA, R. J. and GLASS, D. C. (1985) 'Psychophysiologic correlates of Type A behavior' in *Advances in Behavioral Medicine*, E. S. Katkin and S. B. Manuck (eds), J. A. I., Greenwich, C. T.
12. MATTHEWS, K. A. and HAYNES, S. G. (1986) 'Type A behavior pattern and coronary artery disease: Update and critical evaluation'. *Am. J. Epidemiol.* 123(6): 923.
13. GOODKIN, K., ANTONI, M. H. and BLANEY, P. H. (1986) 'Stress and hopelessness in the promotion of cervical intraepithelial neoplasma to an invasive squamous cell carcinoma of the cervix'. *J. Psychosom. Res.* 30: 67.
14. FRIEDMAN, H. S. and BOOTH-KEWLES, S. (1987) 'The disease-prone personality'. *Am. Psychol.* 42: 534.
15. SPIELBERGER, C. D. et al. (1985) 'The experience and expression of anger: Construction and validation of an Anger Expression Scale' in *Anger and Hostility in Cardio-*

vascular and Behavioural Disorders. M. A. Chesney and R. H. Rosenman (eds), Hemisphere/McGraw-Hill, New York.
16. FRIEDMAN, M. (1969) *Pathogenesis of Coronary Artery Disease*, McGraw-Hill, New York.
17. ROSENMAN, R. H. et al. (1964). 'A Predictive Study of CHD'. *J. Am. Med. Ass.* 189: 15.
18. JENKINS, D. (1971) 'Psychologic and social precursors of coronary disease'. *New Eng. J. Med.* 284: 6, 307.
19. ROSENMAN, R. H. et al. *op. cit.*
20. CAPLAN, R. D. et al (1975) 'Job Demands and worker health: Main effects and Occupational differences'. *NIOSH Research Report*.
21. HOWARD, J. H. et al. (1976) 'Health patterns association with Type A behaviour, a managerial population'. *J. Hum. Stress* vol. 2.
22. FRIEDMAN, M. D. and ROSENMAN, R. H. (1974) *Type A Behaviour and Your Heart*. Knopf, New York.
23. BORTNER, R. W. (1969) 'A short rating scale as a potential measure of pattern A behaviour'. *J. Chron. Dis.* 22: 87.
24. SUINN, R. M. (1975) 'The cardiac stress management program for Type A patients'. *Cardiac Rehabilitation* 5: 12.
25. ROSKIES, E. (1978) 'Considerations in developing a treatment program for the coronary-prone (Type A) behavior pattern' in *Behavior Medicine. Changing Health Life Styles*. P. Davidson (ed), Brunner Mazel, New York.
26. SUINN, R. M. (1978) 'The coronary-prone behavior pattern: A behavioral approach to intervention' in *Coronary-prone behavior*. T. Dembrowski et al. (eds), Springer-Verlag, New York.
27. SUINN, R. M. (1982) 'Intervention with Type A behaviors'. *J. Consulting Psychol.* 50: 933.
28. ROSKIES, E. (1983) 'Stress management for Type A individuals' in *Stress Reduction and Prevention*. D. Melchenbaum and M. Jaremko (eds), New York.
29. JACOB, R. G. and CHESNEY, M. A. (1986) 'Psychological and behavioral methods to reduce cardiovascular reactivity' in *Handbook of stress, reactivity, and cardiovascular disease*. K. A. Matthews, S. M. Weiss, T. Detre, T. M. Dembrowski, B. F.

Falkner, S. B. Manuck and R. B. Williams Jr. (eds), Wiley, New York.
30. MATTHEWS, K. A. and HAYNES, S. G. (1986) 'Type A behavior pattern and coronary artery disease: Update and critical evaluation'. *Am. J. Epidemiol.* 123(6): 923.
31. JACOBSON, E. (1970) *Modern Treatment of Tense Patients*. Charles C. Thomas, Springfield, Ill.
32. BUDZYNISKI, T. (1973) 'Biofeedback procedures in the clinic'. *Seminars in Psychiatry* 5: 537.
33. BARLOW, W. (1977) *The Alexander Technique*. Knopf, New York.
34. HOLLAND PIXIE, 15 Andrews House, Barbican.
35. SCHULTZ, J. H. and LUTHE, W. (1969) *Autogenic Therapy: Autogenic Methods Vol. 1*, Grune & Stratton, New York.
36. EYSENCK, H. J. (1985(a)) 'Personality, cancer and cardiovascular disease: a causal analysis, in *Personality and Individual Differences*. 5: 535.
37. GROSSARTH-MATICEK, R. et al. (1983) 'Psychosomatic factors involved in the process of cancer genesis'. *Psychotherapy and Psychosomatics* 40: 191.
38. GROSSARTH-MATICEK, R. EYSENCK, H. J., VETTER, H. and SCHMIDT, P. (1986) 'Results of the Heidelberg prospective psychomatic intervention study'. Paper presented at the International Conference on Health Psychology, Tilburg University, 3–5 July. 30.
39. KIECOLT-GLASER, J. K. et al. (1984) 'Psychosocial modifiers of immunocompetence in medical students'. *Psychosomatic Medicine* 46: 7–14.
40. BLOOM, B. L. et al. 1987. 'Marital disruption as a stressor: a review and analysis'. *Psychological Bulletin* 85: 867.
41. BLUMENTHAL, M. D. (1967) 'Mental health among the divorced: A field study of divorced and never divorced persons'. *Arch. Gen. Psych.* 16: 603.
42. VERBRUGGE, L.M. (1979) 'Marital status and health'. *J. Marriage. Fam.* 41: 267.
43. SOMERS, A. R. (1979) 'Marital status, health and use of health services'. *JAMA* 241: 1818.
44. BARTROP, R. W. et al. (1977) 'Depressed lymphocyte fraction after bereavement'. *Lancet* i: 834.

45. WINDHOLZ, M. J. et al. (1985) 'A review of the research on conjugal bereavement: Impact on health and efficiency of intervention'. *Comprehensive Psychiatry* 26: 433.
46. *Social Trends 1990* vol. 20. Central Statistical Office, London.
47. *Public Health 1990* Editorial, 104: 153.
48. PENNEBAKER, J. W. et al. (1988) 'Disclosure of traumas and immune function: Health implications for psychotherapy.' *J. Cons. Clin. Psychol.*

10
PERCEPTIONS

If you are sitting alone at home one dark winter's evening, and you hear a sudden, unexpected noise in the room next door, you may well immediately feel afraid and apprehensive, your heart will begin to race and you may come out in a cold sweat. Depending on how brave you are, you either reach for the poker or hide behind the settee. Why is this? What has happened to produce these feelings and reactions in you? They have been produced by what you have thought of the noise, how your brain very quickly analysed and interpreted the noise and its possible consequences. 'It's a burglar. What will he take? Will he come in here next? Will he attack me? What will I do?'

On another occasion, you are again sitting alone at home, and you hear a sudden unexpected noise in the room next door. This time, your thinking is different. Your brain analyses and interprets the noise differently. 'That vase must have fallen. It must have been knocked over by the curtain next to it, blowing in the wind. The children must have left that window open again.' This time your feelings and behaviour are different. You feel annoyed and irritated and your reaction may be to wait until the children return and take them to task.

Your feelings and often your behaviour are governed

by how you perceive or interpret an event or circumstance, and your attitude to it, not by the event or circumstance itself.

Feelings and behaviour do not just come, although many believe they do. They are the product of our thinking, which may sometimes be very fast, almost automatic, or subconscious, as in the case of the sudden noise in the next room.

The sequence of events is:

EVENT→INTERPRETATION→FEELINGS→BEHAVIOUR

Thus one of the most important things governing your reactions to stressors is how you perceive, think about, interpret or see stressors.

How to view stressors

If you see stressors as threats or possible threats to your physical or psychological or spiritual well being, and if you cannot escape from them, the stress they cause can easily go on to cause you harm. If, however, you see stressors as something which cannot harm you or something which you can deal with or overcome, like a challenge, then you will not go on to develop effects of stress.

In other words, it is how you see or perceive or what you think about stressors which decides whether they will get to you or not, not the stressor itself. It was not the noise in the room next door which made you feel afraid or annoyed, but your belief, thinking and interpretation.

Those who view redundancy or even the possibility of redundancy or retirement as a threat to their livelihood, their pride and their reason for living, will feel anxious about the future, and may begin to suffer from the effects of stress. If however, they view these possibilities as opportunities to get out of their present job and begin a new life, they will feel excited, will look forward to the future and will be unlikely to suffer from effects of stress. It is not retirement or redundancy which determines the result, but the attitude to it or how it is seen.

Thinking affects feelings

Sometimes our thinking can be quite contorted without us really realising it, and the result is that we experience unnecessary and damaging feelings.

I heard of a woman who always felt and seemed upset when she was ushered in to see her counsellor. Eventually, the counsellor was able to get from her the thinking that went on in her mind before each session. If her counsellor invited her in a few minutes before the time of her appointment, she thought, 'He wants to get the session over as quickly as possible. He cannot like me.' If the door opened a few minutes late, she thought, 'He is trying to put off and delay seeing me. He cannot like me.' If she was invited in exactly on the dot of her appointment, she thought, 'These sessions are like a conveyor belt, the counsellor does not really like me. It is a purely mechanical process.' It seems obvious to us, reading about this woman, that in fact there were no such hidden motives or feelings on the part of the counsellor and that her thinking was away off beam.

So note also that if your thinking or belief or interpretation of an event of circumstance is wrong in any way, then your feelings and behaviour which follow will be wrong. The change in engine noise when you are flying may in fact be the pilot adjusting the height of the aircraft; if you interpret it as a potential engine fault, then you would be anxious and worry needlessly.

It is extremely important, therefore, that your thinking and your interpretation of stressors is correct. Thus, whenever you experience anxiety or other effects of stress because of a specific stressor or pressure, you should always examine your thinking about that stressor to see if it is correct and reasonable, rational and logical, or if it is wrong, emotional or flawed in any way. If your thinking is wrong, then decide how you can put it right. You *can* change your thinking which will in turn change your feelings. But you *cannot* change your feelings directly. You may want to feel less anxious, but you cannot control the feeling itself. You can only control the thinking that produces the feeling.

Avoid wrong thinking

To begin with, until you become practised in examining your thinking, it is often difficult to see where your thinking is wrong. A look at some examples may help you to start this process of looking critically at your thinking, although you may need help from a wise friend or counsellor to help you in this process.

Some people tend to exaggerate or magnify quite small pressures or stressors into something huge. They make mountains out of molehills. The chance remark by the boss that productivity is down grows in the mind to 'The business must be losing money, it may have to close, I may lose my job', with resulting feelings of fear and anxiety. To these people, a bad weather forecast means bad storm damage and possible financial ruin.

Others take personally everything that is said or everything that happens. The checkout girl who closes just before they reach the till has done it just to spite them—they forget that it may be the end of her shift. They experience feelings of anger and frustration.

Some people are let down by one friend, and enlarge this experience into a fear that nobody can be trusted—the result is feelings of frustration, anger and perhaps helplessness and worthlessness.

Some people, even though they are thanked and praised for what they have done, pick out the few words which they take as criticism and focus on those—they encourage feelings of poor self image and worthlessness.

Some people always believe the worst. If others at a party do not approach and speak to them, they assume that they are disliked and avoided. They forget that the true reason may be that the others are shy and find it easier to speak with people they know. Resulting feelings may be of rejection and poor self worth. To these people, a spot on the skin is never just a pimple, but is bound to be cancer or melanoma with months of pain and death to follow.

And so one could go on with examples of faulty thinking or wrong interpretations. Most of us can remember at least one occasion when a stressor or event produced panic in us, but some see disaster round every corner. People like this are very vulnerable much of the time and they are often liable to suffer from the effects of stress.

If you wish to avoid these stressful feelings, it is important to keep your thinking right. If you already experience damaging feelings, you must correct your wrong thinking.

Get your thinking right

Try to think about pressures rationally without exaggerating them. Do not take events as a personal affront. Take one event for what it is worth—one event—not a reason to begin to make general inferences. Look at things as a whole, the good as well as the bad parts and do not dwell on the bad only. Look for a more optimistic way of viewing an event rather than the most pessimistic.

Remember, you cannot change your feelings directly, you can only change them by changing your thinking.

Summary

1. Feelings and behaviour are a product of our thinking, belief, interpretation of events.
2. Feelings cannot be changed directly, but thinking can be changed and this in turn will change feelings and behaviour.
3. Anxious feelings and fearful behaviour may stem from erroneous thinking so check your thinking.
4. Avoid wrong thinking.
5. Get thinking right.

Further reading

1. *Anxiety Disorders and Phobias: A Cognitive Perspective.* Aaron T. Beck and Gary Emery. Basic Books Inc., New York 1985.
2. *The Practice of Rational-Emotive Therapy.* A. Ellis and W. Dryden. Springer, New York 1987.
3. *Cognitive-Behavioural Counselling in Action.* P. Trower, A. Casey and W. Dryden. Sage Publications, London, 1988.

11
PRACTICAL PRINCIPLES

You have seen in Chapters 7 to 11 how your whole view of life should be changed so that stressors will not produce effects of stress in you.

But what should your practical day to day, moment by moment, approach to successful living be? How should you deal with ongoing circumstances, problems, projects and stressors, and face new ones when they arise, so that you can avoid suffering from the effects of stress?

Stress research has found that people who feel helpless, who think that they are not in control of circumstances but are at the mercy of fate and circumstances and other people, are more likely to suffer from effects of stress. But even those who feel that they are normally in control and therefore are not so vulnerable to stressors, can be overwhelmed by strain when they come up against a stressor or pressure which they cannot actually control.[1-3] And yet, so often, we set *ourselves* objectives over which we have no ultimate control, thus making ourselves very vulnerable.

Impossible objectives

One important principle which you should apply is this: in everything you do every day, never make your overriding objective to change any stressor or achieve anything over which you personally have no ultimate control. Why is this?

If you set yourself an overall objective and achieve it, then you will feel successful. If, however, you set yourself an objective and fail, then you feel frustrated, try harder, become anxious about your failure, and if it has been really important to you, eventually begin to suffer from the effects of stress. If, in addition, you have no ultimate control over achieving the objective, then you have made yourself potentially very vulnerable right from the start. You have set yourself up.

Let us look at this principle in more detail.

First, can you ever completely control another person? You can try to influence him or her, but in the end, if they absolutely refuse to comply, you cannot make them do anything. So you make yourself very vulnerable every time your objective is to change another person. So this principle applies in all circumstances where you are dealing with people or where the stressor is a person, because you have no ultimate control over another person and cannot ever be sure of changing him or her.

From time immemorial, young people contemplating marriage have been advised that they will be very disappointed, and that their marriage may not be successful, if they go into it expecting to change their spouse. And yet many brides' intended progress from the moment they enter the church is 'Aisle, Altar, Hymn' (I'll alter him!). In the same way, we often find ourselves in situations where we set out to change another person's mind or attitude or behaviour. If they change, we are pleased and feel successful; if they do not (and we have never any ultimate control over whether they will or not) then we get frustrated. We may try harder to make them change—all the time, probably, making them resist the more—and then, if this has really been important to us,

PRACTICAL PRINCIPLES 97

we become anxious about our failure and eventually may show signs of the effects of stress.

So do not risk it. Do not make your overriding objectives to change anyone.

The situation is similar if we are dealing with stressors or with circumstances. There are few occasions in life when you hold all the aces or can pull all the strings. You are seldom in ultimate control. If you set yourself objectives for these situations and achieve them, all is well. But if you fail, then you may slip into stress and from the start you make yourself very vulnerable.

So what then can you do? How can you have objectives which you can ultimately control, despite people or circumstances beyond your control?

Achievable objectives

The second principle is that two objectives are always within your control:
 to do your best,
 to do what is right.
If you make these your objectives, rather than changing people or circumstances or achieving things, then you cannot fail.

Let us examine this principle in more detail. If your objective is to do your best and to do what is right, then you cannot fail because of someone else's actions. You are in charge, you are always in control, and achieving your objective is in your hands. You need never, therefore, get frustrated, because you need never fail. You need never become anxious or suffer from effects of stress because you have not been able to change a stressor.

Moreover, if you get your thinking and attitudes and actions right in this way, it is surprising how often the person or situation does change without you trying to bring about the change. A few examples may illustrate this important principle.

If you have a wayward or a difficult spouse, it is natural that you would like them to change, to be more understanding, to stop behaving as they do, to start loving you again, to stop drinking, and so on. However, you have no real control over whether they will change or not; often the harder you try to get them to change the more resistant and difficult they become. You then try even harder, they resist more, you become frustrated, and eventually you begin to suffer from the effects of stress.

The principle is that you must do what is right and do your best to be a good husband or wife. Remember, the reason is not so that your spouse will change but because what you are doing is right, and what is expected of a good spouse. Any change in them is not your responsibility in the end because you have no control over them.

Suppose your objective at work is promotion. Perhaps you are not promoted but are passed over, maybe more than once. Then you try harder to merit promotion, to bring yourself to your boss's attention, perhaps even belittling others in the process. You may become suspicious or even paranoid about the matter; you may feel a failure; in the end you become bitter and resentful with possibly other effects of stress developing in you. You have made yourself vulnerable because you have chosen an objective over which you have no ultimate control. Even if you have worked hard and well, your boss, for his own reasons, may prefer someone else.

Your objective at work should not be promotion, but to do your best and to do what is right. If promotion comes, that is wonderful, but if not you won't suffer from effects of stress as a result.

Perhaps you are a sportsman or woman: your goal is to win. If you do not win you can become discouraged and depressed, eventually feel a failure and begin to suffer from the effects of stress. You have made yourself vulnerable because, no matter how well you run or play, someone may do better and win: in the end you have no control over the situation. Your goal should always be to do your best and to do what is right; then you cannot lose and need never feel a failure, need never feel really depressed. Of course, you may feel disappointed and down for a little while when you lose; this is only natural. But if winning has not been your goal, then you will not be devastated by not winning.

If you have a difficult child your objective may be to change the child's behaviour. When the behaviour does not change, you try harder and get involved in power struggles, feel frustrated and angry, and eventually begin to feel some effects of stress. You cannot force the child to change, because you cannot control that, so you have made yourself very vulnerable. Rather, your objective should be to do what is right and to do your best as a parent. You must put these principles into practice, not to change the child, but because it is right. Strangely, when your attitude changes in this way, often the child's behaviour changes too, and often quite quickly.

So your objective in all that you do or are involved in, should be to do your best and to do what is right.

Things have purpose

The third principle is that you should look on everything that happens to you as having a purpose. People who do this are much less likely to suffer from the effects of stress than those who believe that fate or luck or life is fickle and has it in for them.

Sometimes it is possible to see that some good may come out of really difficult circumstances: a broken leg, though painful, may produce an enforced rest and slowing down which may be a blessing in disguise. At other times, it is possible to believe that some good may come in the future from what, at the time, seem large pressures. Failing in an exam or in another task may bring you back to earth with a resolve to study, practice or work harder in the future.

If you can believe that 'no matter what', good will come, then you are less likely to suffer from strain. So it is important that you try to believe that all things—all stressors—have a purpose.

Summary

1. Do not set yourself objectives which are beyond your control.
2. Make sure that your overriding objectives in everything are to do your best, and to do what is right.
3. Believe that all things have a purpose and work for your good.

Notes

1. ROTTER, J. B. (1966) 'Generalised expectations for internal versus external control of reinforcement'. *Psychology Monograph vol. 80*.
2. PECK, D. and WHITLOW, D. (1975) *Approaches to Personality Theory*. Methuen, London.
3. COOPER, C. L. et al. (1988) *Living with Stress*. Penguin, London.

12
THE SPIRIT

Parts of a whole

In many 'holistic' approaches to stress management the importance of the mind (or soul) and body is recognised.[1,2] However, it is accepted—certainly by our Maker—that we are made up of three parts: spirit, soul,

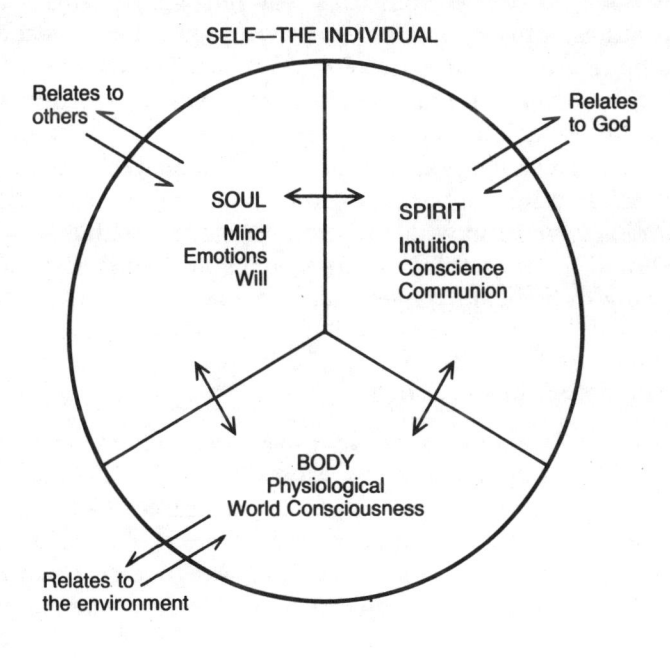

```
                SELF—THE INDIVIDUAL

    Relates to                          Relates
    others                              to God

              SOUL  ⟷  SPIRIT
              Mind       Intuition
              Emotions   Conscience
              Will       Communion


                    BODY
                 Physiological
              World Consciousness

    Relates to
    the environment
```

and body.[3-6] It is important, therefore, that we adopt a 'wholistic approach' where all three aspects are dealt with.

Each part affects the other. Aristotle recognised this—at least partially:

> Soul and body, as it seems to me, are affected sympathetically by one another: on the one hand, an alteration in the state of the soul produces an alteration in the form of the body and, contrariwise, an alteration in the bodily form produces an alteration in the state of the soul.[7]

If we feel afraid of the future because of anxious thinking (in our soul), this may contribute to an ulcer or high blood pressure (in our body). On the other hand, if we suffer constant pain (in our body), this can make us feel depressed (in our soul), in turn breaking our spirit. If we are dried up spiritually (in our spirit), this can produce depression in our souls with a knock-on effect of fatigue and lassitude (in our body).

So if we are going to give ourselves the best opportunity of dealing with stressors, it is important that each part is functioning at its best level.[6] So far we have dealt with keeping the body in good shape, (by exercise, diet and lifestyle) and with our soul (particularly with how we should learn to think if our feelings and behaviour are going to be healthy). We must now deal with the spirit.

The nature of the spirit

Christian teaching is that man was originally made to be dependent upon God, his Creator, (Jn 15:5; 3:8, 9) and his human spirit was able to communicate directly with God (Gen 1:27; 2:7). Man was created primarily as a spiritual being, with a soul and body, and designed to perform with his spirit in ascendancy over his soul and body, resulting in harmony of functioning. However, man (Adam) decided to go his own way rather than God's, because he thought that he could operate independently of God (Gen 3:4–7). The consequence was that although his human spirit still existed, God cut it off from himself: in fact it was then dead to God (Matt 8:22; Eph 2:1). Man's spirit still functions within him, but in ways that are totally opposed to God's ways and purposes, and at odds with the way man was designed to operate and function. This dead spirit has far-reaching impact on the ways our soul and body function, and they too suffer the consequences of our spirit's malfunctioning (Gen 3).

Being totally just and holy, God could not forgive man for what he had done, and so man's spiritual relationship with him could not be restored (Rom 5:18). Instead, God had to create a totally new, blameless, human spirit in man, and this could only be achieved by God's Son Jesus Christ, coming to earth as a man, dying in man's place for what he had originally done wrong, and being raised up from the dead (2 Cor 5:14,15). Anyone who availed himself of this transaction would be 'born again'—of the Spirit of God—he would be given a totally new spirit (Jn 3:6; Ezek 36:26).

So if our spirit is to function as intended, we in fact need a new spirit, and this can be ours if we follow certain steps.

How to be born again

Jesus said 'You must be born again.' The offer of a new birth is conditional on your agreeing with and accepting the following:

that Jesus Christ is the Son of God;
that he came to earth as a man to die on the cross for me and that he rose again from the dead;

that I have been going my own way rather than God's way;

that I want to turn from any wrong that I have done and from my selfish ways and to surrender all that I am and have and all that I shall be to God;

If you truly believe and agree with the above you should:

now accept God's forgiveness;

now accept a new spirit and the Holy Spirit to live in your spirit.

Because it is a new creation, this new spirit is perfect. It is therefore not guilty as far as the past is concerned, and cannot be found guilty in the future (Rom 8:1, 33–35), and it will live forever with God. It is able to communicate directly with God (Rom 8:14–17). Moreover, God's Spirit, the Holy Spirit, takes up residence in this new human spirit (Rom 8:9). Our spirit is then ready to function as designed.

Health warning!

It is important to realise that having learned this and understood it, if you then do not decide to take the steps outlined above, your human spirit will remain dead to God. This will be your permanent condition if you do not ever take these steps towards God, continuing on after physical death into eternity. Moreover, things will never be the same again. You will be more accountable to God—having heard, understood and then rejected his offer to restore you to a relationship with him—than you would have been if you had never heard this great news.

In other words, reading this chapter and taking no action can damage your health!

References

1. PELLETIER, K. R. (1977) *Mind as healer, mind as slayer: A holistic approach to preventing stress disorders*. Dell, New York.
2. CURTIS, J. D. and DETERT, R. A. (1981) *How to relax: A holistic approach to stress management*. Mayfield Publishing Co., Palo Alto, Calif.
3. 1 Thessalonians 5: 23.
4. MINIRTH, F. B. (1977) *Christian Psychiatry*, Fleming H. Revell Co., Old Tappan, N.J.
5. MUNRO, W. S. (1989) 'Religious belief and stress: A review of cognitive and behaviour stress coping strategies inherent in religious belief' in *Stress and Tension Control—Stress Management 3*. McGuigan, Sime, Macdonald Wallace (eds), Plenum Press, New York & London.
6. REED, W. S. (1979) *Healing the Whole Man, Body, Mind & Spirit*. Fleming H. Revell Co., Old Tappan, N.J.
7. ARISTOTLE. *De Anima*

Part Three

The Real Secret

13
INTRODUCTION TO A CLOSED BOOK

If you want to get the most out of your car or computer, and to know what to do if something goes wrong with it, you are wise to consult the maker's manual or handbook rather than other doubtful sources—people who may be experts or even famous in their own field but who know little of the maker's designs.

In Part Three we will apply your Maker's secrets, contained in the Bible, to the important factors identified in Part Two as responsible for making you less vulnerable to pressures (2 Tim 3:16,17).

These secrets, however, are not for everyone. They will remain a closed book or mystery to you unless the Maker makes them clear to you (Jn 12:38–40; 2 Cor 4:3,4). He can only do this if you have been 'born again' (see Chapter 12) so that God's Holy Spirit can now be living in your spirit. It is His Holy Spirit who will make these things clear to you (1 Cor 2:10).

So I recommend that before reading any further you pray now: 'My Maker and my God, in Jesus' name, I ask that your Holy Spirit opens the eyes of my mind, so that I will understand and appreciate the secrets of living as you designed me to, as set out in your Book' (Ps 119:18).

Deal with stressors

You should start by reviewing the stressors, the external pressures in your life, and then try to analyse what exactly it is about them which causes your problems. Then you can begin to deal with these factors where it is in your power to do so.

You may need help with the analysis and decisions about what can be done to lessen these external pressures on yourself. While a trusted friend or (better still) a trained counsellor can often help you to see more clearly, we would always recommend that you pray about your stress. Ask that God will himself put his finger on the main problem areas, and then show you with the help of his manual what to do about them. Sometimes, God may use a Christian counsellor to pinpoint these areas.

We saw in Chapter 3 that it is particularly important that you admit to yourself which stressors you have inflicted on yourself, before ruthlessly dealing with them. It is not easy for many of us to be completely honest, and God realises this, and we ourselves are aware deep down if we stop to think that we have been deluding ourselves (Jer 17:9,10). The Manual has a good deal to say about self-inflicted stressors and their consequences—the dishonest practices (Prov 20:23, Eph 4:28), financial committments (Eph 5:5,6), irresponsible behaviour (Eph 5:15–17, Prov 23:29–35, 5:1–14), extramarital affairs (Exod 20:14, Matt 5:27,28), and over ambition (Prov 23:4,5, Ecc 4:4, Gal 5:26).

One of the most subtle self-inflicted stressors is simply taking on too much: subtle, because many of the things we take on are worthwhile, useful, help others, may be religious, and may even be God's work, and if we don't do them, who will? However, this can be a quick route to the effects of stress, nervous breakdown, or a heart attack, and the over-committed schedule gives us up, before we can give it up. See what Solomon thought of being a philanthropist and workaholic (Ecc 1:4–10).

14
FINDING SUPPORT

In Chapter 4 we discovered that there are two big moderators of stressors: support, and the nature of the individual. In Chapter 5 we saw the role of support in helping people to withstand stressors. Your Manual highlights this need for support. We are told to help one another and that we need each other (Ecc 4:9–12). There is advice also to wives to support their husbands (Col 3:18; 1 Pet 3:1,2; Eph 5:22–24) and for husbands to love their wives (Col 3:19; Eph 5:25–29). We saw the importance of this in preventing men from developing heart attacks and women from developing depression. The Bible goes further than just support, however. It says we should love one another (Jn 13:34). This is usually taken as a command. However, we all need to receive love and so you should accept as much love as is available.

Find a supportive church

Often when we offer to put people in touch with a church where we know they will receive all the support they need, we are met with a certain lack of enthusiasm. Many remember the church they were taken to as children, and other churches they have known, where everyone appeared to be in control of themselves and their lives: 'Good morning' and 'Good night' were the only words of support ever heard, and support was offered only when someone died.

But our Maker does mean us to have support from a local extended family—the church. He has told the members of the church that they should help each other whenever necessary (Gal 6:2). In his scheme of things the local church should contain all the types of support which may be needed, not just spiritual support (Rom 12:4–21).

The church to which my wife and I belong takes this literally, and is always generous with its support. God supplies the resources for whatever help is required. There is a fund for those who need financial help over a temporary difficulty; help is available from one of the accountants in the church to plan finances and budgets; others offer to help with babysitting and child minding to give mothers a break from the constant demands of bringing up a young family; there is physical help with shopping, cleaning and gardening for ailing and older members; moral support for single parents; psychological support for those going through testing times; and spiritual support and direction for all.

If you are not a churchgoer, have you thought of looking for a supportive church? Nowadays there are many churches like this. Just knowing that support is available is good for us, and it makes us feel loved, wanted and cared for. The support may be given at Sunday or other special services, by teams of counsellors, or at weekly housegroups where small groups of trusted church members are able to support each other; individuals also support their friends in the 'family'.

But it is not enough to know that such churches exist and can help; it is important that you overcome inertia, make the effort to find one and, having found it, be open enough to explain your needs and then be willing to accept the support given. If you are a churchgoer and in a position to give support to others, then it is very important that you do not hold back. If your church is not one which goes out of its way to support those who need it, then you must ask why? We have been told to support one another (Gal 6:2).

Do not be too proud to seek and accept support. It will help prevent you developing effects of stress.

Beware bogus support

In Chapter 5 we discussed the dangers of coming to rely on alcohol, cigarettes, tranquillisers and overeating. The Manual warns against over-indulgence in alcohol (Prov 23:29–35; Eph 5:18) but also appears to recognise that in moderation it is all right, and even good for us (1 Tim 5:23, Prov 31:6,7).

While the Manual does not say anything specifically about smoking—the habit had not started then—it does warn us of the effects of harming our bodies (1 Cor 3:16,17), and there is now no doubt at all in the medical world that smoking does harm us. The Bible also warns us of the dangers of things that we cannot do without, and their importance in our lives, and certainly smoking is an addictive habit (Exod 20:3,4).

15
FIT FOR LIFE

As we saw in Part Two, a number of factors about the individual are moderators of stressors, and fitness is an important one. Those who are fit are less likely to let stressors affect them.

Perhaps we should not be surprised that the Bible, written 2,000 to 4,000 years ago, deals with all the factors which we now believe are important because, after all, God made us, so he should know.

Exercise

Exercise is important in keeping fit. Your Maker's Manual does recommend physical training as having some benefit (1 Tim 4:8). There was probably little need for detailed advice on taking enough exercise, as the people of those days were much more active than we are now. In Biblical times walking great distances was a regular part of life. For example, the disciples on the way to Emmaus walked seven miles from Jerusalem to Emmaus, and then walked seven miles back again that same night after having met the resurrected Lord Jesus (Lk 24:13,33,34).

Weight watching

Keeping a reasonable weight keeps you fit and helps you to feel more confident. Your Maker's Manual warns you not to eat too much (Prov 23:2; 23:20,21).

Diet

Avoid sweet things. Your Manual warns us not to eat too much honey (Prov 25:16,27).

Cut down on the fatty, greasy foods. We have realised only recently the harm animal fat can bring to our arteries; the Manual, written 4,000 to 5,000 years ago, advises the Israelites that they should avoid eating animal fat. This is in the Old Testament and thought by some not directly applicable nowadays. Nevertheless it is interesting, especially since it says that this practice should be for all generations to come! (Lev 3:17; 7:22–24).

16
CHANGING LIFESTYLE

In Chapter 7 we explored the importance of an individual's healthy lifestyle in making him resistant to stressors.

Rest, relaxation and sleep

These are important in sufficient quantity. Your Maker's Manual tells you that you should give one day in seven to God (Exod 20:10,11; 31:14–17), and God himself rested on the seventh day when he was busy creating the world (Gen 2:2,3).

Since I became a Christian, my own experience and that of many others has been that, if we give one day in seven to God, all the work is done in time and there is sufficient money to go round, apparently miraculously. The Manual advises against *overwork* which we take on because we are afraid that we will not have sufficient to eat (Ps 27:2). Moreover, we feel more refreshed and ready to go when Monday morning comes round. Many in the caring professions—ministers, church leaders, doctors, nurses, social workers, counsellors and others—who have a full-time job but are also engaged in voluntary work, fill each day in the week with work of one kind or another and are wearing themselves out. They too need to take one day off in seven to relax with their family or friends.

An important lesson from the Manual concerns the Lord Jesus himself. He had only three years to accomplish all that had to be done, and he was in constant demand as a teacher, prophet and leader. Yet he took time off and went away by himself or with his closest friends to rest and relax, as well as to spend time with God (Mk 6:31,32). He did not attempt to do everything. He even sometimes said 'No'. He did only what God wanted him to do (Jn 5:19; 6:38). Is there not a lesson for us here?

Many gifts of God, such as music, poetry, art, literature, and the beauty of the natural world help us to relax. When King Saul was anxious and distraught he sent for a musician to soothe him, and David often played his harp to this effect (1 Sam 16:23). The Maker's Manual advises that we spend time thinking about good and lovely things (Phil 4:8). Live one day at a time (Matt 6:34).

Meditation

Meditation is a well-known method of relaxation, but should be handled with care. We believe that there can be spiritual dangers in certain forms of it, such as transcendental meditation.

However, Biblical meditation—meditating on God's word—was recommended several thousands of years ago as being good for us (Ps 1:1,2). Why not take the Maker's Manual's advice rather than that of some pop star, television personality, or leader of some religious cult? Some help is needed to enable people to develop this practice, and there are a number of excellent books available on this subject (such as Campbell McAlpine's *The Practice of Biblical Meditation*).

Delegate

There are many examples of delegation in the Maker's Manual. Right at the beginning, God delegated the naming of the animals to Adam (Gen 2:19,20); and when things were getting on top of Moses, his father-in-law suggested that he should delegate (Exod 18:13–27).

Although he could have done everything himself, Jesus himself delegated many things to his disciples and others—for instance, when he gave tasks to the disciples before he fed the five thousand (Lk 9:12–17). Should we not learn from all this?

Planning priorities

Most people do not make conscious decisions about life's big priorities, sometimes with tragic consequences. We urged you to decide on who and what is really important to you and then to give them the time, energy and importance they deserve.

But supposing you do stop and think—how are you to decide on your priorities when there are conflicting demands for your attention, affection, time, and energy? Who and what should come first? Do you choose according to how you feel at the time, or by who makes the biggest play for your attention? If you get it wrong, you do so at your peril, either of losing what you hold dear, or of continuing conflict and pressure on you which may lead to effects of stress.

The Maker's Manual, I believe, is quite clear about priorities. If you ignore these or make up your own list, then you need not be surprised if things go wrong. It is comforting to have this clear guidance and if you follow it you know you are functioning as our Maker intends us to function. Do not be tempted to change it without good reason.

Put God First—and remember that this is not the same

as going to church or doing good things. It means that you must have time to spend with God, and put his will before yours in everyday life (Matt 22:37; Exod 20:3).

Next comes your spouse (Eph 5:22,25; Gen 2:24; Mal 2:15)—he or she comes before your children or your ageing parents, and certainly before your work and other activities, even the most noble and laudable. Next come your children (Mk 6:36; Eph 6:4; Matt 18:5,6; Mal 2:15) these must come before work.

Your family and parents do have a claim on you, according to the Maker's Manual, and you must honour them and look after them (1 Tim 5:8; Eph 6:2)—but not before God, spouse and children.

Next, consider your work. You have a responsibility to your employer, or to those who pay you, and you must respect them. The Maker's Manual is very clear about your responsibilities in this and you must observe them (Col 3:22–25).

Only after all these do we come to church activities; it is well to think about this. If you are involved in them, worthy as they are, make sure that they are not rising further up the priority list than they should (Matt 15:4–6; Lk 10:38–42; Mk 7:10–13). If they do, then you are not doing what the Maker's Manual advises; you should not be surprised if problems arise which may lead to the effects of stress, not only in yourself but in members of your family. It is tragic that we often read nowadays of church leaders (for whom church and work may well be the same), who put these two items way up on their priority list, often before children, or even spouse, and even sometimes God. The sad consequences are broken families, divorce, burn-out and effects of stress in themselves, in colleagues and in family members.

Other good works come after your loyalty and responsibility to your church and church activities. Last of all you may give time to your own 'selfish' concerns (Phil 2:3,4).

Further reading

1. *The Practice of Biblical Meditation*. Campbell McAlpine. Marshall, Morgan & Scott, London, 1981.
2. *Seconds Away*. David Cormack, MARC Europe, 1986.

17
A NEW IDENTITY

Your true value

In Chapter 8 we saw that those who believe in themselves and are committed to what they are doing deal well with stressors. We saw that a poor self image can often be traced back to our early formative years and our continuing belief that we are failures. Our real worth, however, is not in what we have achieved, but in who we are.

However, there are some people who despite affirmation and being told that they are intrinsically worthwhile, just cannot believe that they are of any value at all. They feel a failure, unloved, unwanted and rejected. They appear shy, defeated, and pathetic, and apologise for all they do—almost for taking up space on the planet.

If you are one of these defeated and worthless people and feel that the only way would be for you to start all over again, then there is good news. The Maker's Manual's view is that you are potentially very worthwhile (Jn 3:16). You can be changed. You can obtain a brand new spirit. You can have a new beginning. If you have taken the steps described in Chapter 12, then you have been born again (Jn 3:3–7).

You are of untold value and worth in your Creator's

eyes. You are a son and heir of God; a member of God's royal family and a brother of the Lord Jesus Christ (Rom 8:15–17; Eph 1:3–5, 2:19; 1 Jn 5:1). That is your true image and it does not depend on anything that you have accomplished or achieved; God sees you as a wonderful new being. So what does it really matter what other people think about you or say about you? Moreover, God has totally forgiven you for all your past, and so there is no need for any more guilt on your part (1 Jn 1:9; Col 1:14, 2:13).

Where is the need for you to have a poor self image ever again? You can hold your head up high. You are really worthwhile and you are totally forgiven.

Value your work

As far as commitment is concerned, the Maker's Manual agrees that you should be totally committed to whatever you do. It is good for you. You have been made to be totally dedicated and committed to the furtherance of God's kingdom—in you, in others and in the world (Mk 8:34–37; Matt 6:31–33, 10:37–39).

Crucial needs

We saw also in Chapter 8 that if you cannot depend completely on your sources for meeting your deepest needs, for love and security, significance and value, then you are vulnerable and must be prepared to lose them with potentially devastating results.

We always invite those who attend our seminars to look at their lives and sometimes we have to help them to clarify matters in their own minds. Having established on what or on whom they are relying for these needs, we then ask 'How dependable are they? How much control do you have over these sources? Can you really control whether your wife loves you?—Of course, you can do all the things that will make it more likely that she will but, in the end, if she says "I don't love you any more," can you change her mind if she has made it up?' They see that they have no ultimate control.

Then we ask similar questions about other areas. 'Have you control over your job? Is it absolutely secure? No chance of nationalisation, privatisation, takeover? Change of boss who may think that you do not fit in? Redundancy? You may work hard and conscientiously and be really good at your job but, in the end, can you be absolutely sure that it will continue as it has been?' Most admit that they have no ultimate control.

'Have you control over whether your husband or wife, or friends or colleagues say things to you which will make you feel good—or at least not make you feel put down?' A little reflection shows them that again the answer is 'No'.

It is not long before almost everyone admits that they are getting love and security and significance from sources over which they have no ultimate control. To drive matters home, we ask 'Is there anything or anybody that you have control over?' Quite a number say 'No. Nothing and nobody—only ourselves.'

'Really? You cannot be sure that you will not fall ill, have an accident, even die. Do you control your life? Can you be sure of living one more day? Can you prevent yourself losing one hair of your head, going bald, going grey, growing old?' (Lk 12:16-25). The answer again is 'No.' And a number of those people whom we have been trying to help then say, 'This is really depressing.'

What we have shown them, I hope, is that they are relying on sources over which they have no ultimate control for meeting deep needs of love and security and significance. They have made themselves totally and utterly vulnerable. At any time, the sources can be taken away or destroyed, and those unmet needs lead sometimes quite swiftly to fear, anxiety, loss of self esteem, and a host of other effects of stress. It certainly is a depressing thought when it sinks home.

Meeting your deepest needs

However, the Maker's Manual as ever has the answer (Jer 2:13,18). God tells us that he is the one to slake our deep thirsts and longings alone; but that we have abandoned him, the spring of living water, and have sought to meet our deepest needs from sources of our own making (broken cisterns). We also seek satisfaction from other 'rivers' (v. 18), which, while giving us relief for a time, are ultimately undependable and will let us down and betray us at some time or other.

You have been made to be utterly dependent on God. All your deepest needs have to be met by and through him and he is utterly dependable (Phil 4:19; Heb 13:8). If, as he advises, your love and security come from him, and your significance comes from what you are in his sight, then you can never again be completely vulnerable.

True, God may provide part of your love and security and significance through other human beings and things —your spouse and family, your job, and so on. Loss of these human agents may well produce a degree of understandable grief, concern or hurt. This is normal, and you should not pretend that you do not hurt or feel guilty because you do hurt. Instead, tell your heavenly Father that you do. Denying or supressing a sense of loss or concern or hurt can eventually lead to effects of stress (see Chapters 9 and 19). However, as long as the bottom line and ultimate source of your deepest needs is God, you will not be devastated and you will not end with catastrophic effects of stress. St Paul said

We are hard pressed on every side, but not crushed; perplexed, but not in 'despair'; persecuted, but not abandoned; struck down, but not destroyed.

Further reading

1. *Inside Out*. Dr Lawrence J. Crabb. Navpress, Colorado Springs, 1988.

18
A CHANGE OF ATTITUDE

In Chapter 9 we looked at different types of personality and their vulnerabilities. The go-getting Type A is likely to develop high blood pressure and a heart attack or stroke if he does not slow down. However, Type As often find it difficult to relax or change their behaviour, and what is required is a basic change in attitude. The Maker's Manual advises a change in fundamental attitudes, a whole new outlook on life, which then changes behaviour (Rom 12:2).

If you consider that your value as a person lies in your relationship to God, (as the Manual says it should be) and not in status, position or wealth, then your attitude to striving is bound to change (Phil 4:19; Mk 8:36; 1 Tim 6:17; Lk 12:14–21). If you believe, as the Manual says, that God has a plan for your life (Jer 29:11; Eph 1:9,10), then your attitude to trying to achieve will change. If you believe that the timing of events is ultimately in God's hands (Ps 31:14,15; Eph 1:11) and not yours, then your attitude to deadlines and time pressures will change. If you believe that the meek shall inherit the earth (Matt 5:5) and that God is in ultimate charge of your future and destiny, then your attitude to aggression and hostility will change. If you believe that you can trust God fully, then you will not worry unduly about income or your daily needs. God will supply them (Lk 12:31).

After all, Jesus said,

> So my counsel is: don't worry about *things*—food, drink, money and clothes. For you already have life and a body—and they are far more important than what to eat and wear. Look at the birds! They don't worry about what to eat—they don't need to sow or reap or store up food—for your heavenly Father feeds them. And you are far more valuable to him than they are. Will all your worries add a single moment to your life? And why worry about your clothes? Look at the field lilies. They don't worry about theirs. Yet King Solomon in all his glory was not clothed as beautifully as they. And if God cares so wonderfully for flowers that are here today and gone tomorrow, won't he more surely care for you, O men of little faith? So don't worry at all about having enough food and clothing. Why be like the heathen? For they take pride in all these things and are deeply concerned about them. But your heavenly Father already knows perfectly well that you need them. And he will gladly give them to you if you give him first place in your life. So don't be anxious about tomorrow. God will take care of your tomorrow too. Live one day at a time (Matt 6:25-34, Living Bible).

If you accept the advice of the Maker's Manual about rest and relaxation, then you will learn to relax and take time off.

Healthy emotions

People who bear resentments and bitterness may develop forms of rheumatoid arthritis and other chronic conditions. 'Your attitudes to past hurts must change' is the advice of the Maker's Manual. You should always forgive and love instead (Mk 11:25), and if you do so you are less likely to suffer from certain chronic conditions as a result of stressors in your life.

People who bottle up emotions or who often feel hopeless and helpless are vulnerable to some forms of cancer. Your Maker's Manual advises that you should not be afraid of your emotions, that you should be happy with others when they are happy, and if they are sad you should share their sorrow (Rom 12:15). You are advised to be totally open with God about how you feel. If you can be sure of being surrounded by God's love and care, then you need not feel hopeless and helpless (Heb 13:5, 6; Deut 31:6; Ps 23:1–6).

Lowered immunity can develop in the lonely with subsequent development of effects of stress. Your Maker's Manual teaches that you need never be alone (Matt 28:20), that Jesus loves you and has made it possible for you to enjoy a personal and intimate relationship with him, banishing the deepest loneliness, and will look after you in this life, and that you can have a wonderful hope for eternity to come (Lk 18:29,30). You can be sure of spending it with God in total harmony and without any fear (Eph 1:9–14; Rom 6:5–10).

Openness and confession

Hidden emotions make some people more vulnerable to stressors with a danger of psychosomatic illnesses, anxieties and phobias developing when they are faced with stressors. Hidden emotions should be uncovered: ask God to reveal these to you. This can also be done with a Christian counsellor during a prayer time. Facing your problems and your feelings of guilt makes you feel stronger and increases your immunity; the Roman Catholic church has always encouraged confession, and this can be a powerful release of tension and pressure. The Apostle James advises that you should 'confess your sins to each other, and pray for each other so that you may be healed' (Jas 5:16).

There may be times, however, when other people are not available, or when it may not be appropriate for us to go to others. The Manual encourages us to open up to God himself 'pray all the time. Ask God for anything in line with the Holy Spirit's wishes. Plead with him, reminding him of your needs ...' (Eph 6:18, Living Bible). 'If we confess our sins, he ... will forgive us' (1 Jn 1:9). But apart from confessing we should also simply speak to him as a father, telling him and admitting to him our fears, aspirations and misgivings. 'Don't worry about anything; instead, pray about everything; tell God your needs and don't forget to thank him for his answers' (Phil 4:6, Living Bible). 'Your Father knows what you need before you ask him' (Matt 6:8). 'Let him have all your worries and cares, for he is always thinking about you and watching everything that concerns you.' (1 Pet 5:7, Living Bible).

Speaking to God knowing that he understands all about you, that he will hear you, that he loves you and will answer your prayers, must surely have a greater effect on your immunity and health than merely writing about your problems as the students did in Chapter 9, or even than opening up to a mere human psychologist.

Jesus said 'Come to me, all you who are weary and burdened, and I will give you rest' (Matt 11:28). So do not bottle up your anxieties and problems. Share them with a Christian friend, or counsellor, or pastor. Tell God himself about them, discuss them with him and leave them with him.

19
CHRISTIAN THINKING

We saw in Chapter 10 that one of the most important factors which determines an individual's vulnerability to stressors is how he views them, his thinking about them and his interpretation of them. We saw that it is important to avoid wrong thinking, because thinking controls our feelings and behaviour.

How you think is of utmost importance: for the most part it is wrong and foolish (Rom 1:21, 22). It is imperative therefore that it is changed to fall into line with God's way of thinking (Rom 12:2).

What about the Christian view of stressors? We have already seen that you should review them to see which you have brought on yourself and can either avoid or change. What should your thinking be, though, about the unavoidable stressors in your life? How should your thinking change so that these stressors cannot have a harmful effect on you? Here are some ways.

A Christian perspective

If you have taken the steps outlined in Chapter 12 and are born again, then not only are you forgiven and have a new spirit but also God has promised that you will spend eternity with him, where stressors will never bother you again. You will live with him in perfect peace and contentment (Jn 14:1-4). If you think about this for a moment, you soon get the stressors in your life into perspective. Even the large ones (let alone the small ones which you seem to worry about) become insignificant in the light of the hope that you have for the future. Even when it seems that these stressors will not go away and that they will last for ever, you can begin to see them as short episodes in a relatively short life on this earth, compared with an eternal life with God.

A few decades ago, there was much more preaching from pulpits and more hymns sung about heaven and about how wonderful it would be—probably because life here was pretty miserable for many, and the hope to come was very important. Nowadays life for most people is much easier, so the balance in preaching has swung to a better life now. But this future hope should not be forgotten when things at present seem bleak.

Trust excludes fear

If you have been born again and have received a new spirit, then the Manual tells you that God is your Father. You can be sure that you are surrounded by his love and his protection and that he will never leave you. If you think about this, then you need fear no stressor on earth—not even death itself, let alone any lesser ones (Rom 8:34-39).

If you are totally trusting God in this life and for the life to come, then how desperate are the present stressors? It is important to remind yourself that you cannot be fully trusting God and be feeling anxious at the same time. You can be trusting God at 9.00 am and therefore you cannot be feeling anxious. At 9.15 am you can be feeling anxious but, if you are, you are not trusting God entirely at 9.15 am. Anxiety can be unbelief in disguise.

If, therefore, you are ever feeling unduly anxious about stressors, you have to realise that your thinking must be wrong. You need to ask yourself, 'What is my thinking here? Am I trusting God in this problem, and if not, why not?' Then you must proceed to change your thinking about trusting God entirely. If you do so, feelings of anxiety about stressors will go. Remember, feelings cannot be changed directly, they can only be changed by changing your thinking.

Constructive thinking

Your thinking should be 'This stressor has come so that I will become more dependent upon God.' In other words, you should take your attention away from the stressor and turn it on God. If you use stressors in this constructive way, then God will cause the stressor to shrink in size or even to change or disappear. Remember, if you turn your face to the sun, your shadow will fall behind you.

Getting our thinking right as Christians is not easy, because we all tend to be very aware of our emotions rather than our thinking. However, the Manual says 'as a man thinketh so is he' (Prov 23:7, AV) and also tells us that we should be 'transformed by the renewing of our minds' (Rom 12:2, NIV). So it is important that you examine your thinking to see if it is in line with what the Manual says it should be. If it is not, make sure that you change it in whatever way necessary. You may need help at the beginning to see where your thinking is wrong, and to find guidance in putting it right. You can do this by asking God to show you, or by seeking help from a Christian counsellor. Jesus said, 'and you will know the truth, and the truth will set you free' (Jn 8:32).

Further reading

1. *Effective Biblical Counselling*. Lawrence J. Crabb. Marshall, Morgan & Scott, 1985.

20
APPLYING GOD'S PRINCIPLES

In our exploration of ways to beat stress, we discussed several important principles. The first was that you should avoid setting objectives over which you have no ultimate control, such as trying to change people or situations. The second was that you should aim instead to do your best and to do what is right, in all circumstances. If you make these your objectives rather than changing people or circumstances or achieving things, then you cannot fail.

Pleasing God

Christian teaching does not contradict this but goes further. The Maker's Manual says that your main objective should be how best you can please God in the situation and in dealing with the stressor. But 'seek first his kingdom and his righteousness, and all these things will be given to you as well' (Matt 6:33; Lk 12:31). 'Whatever you do, do it all for the glory of God' (1 Cor 10:31). You must do what will please him irrespective of the outcome in any given situation.

How do you know what will please him? First, he has given very clear instructions in general terms in the Maker's Manual about what will please him. Secondly, he has also given specific details of what will please him in many problem areas. We have touched on some of these already, when discussing our priorities.

If you are looking for guidance on specific subjects, you might like to consult the Bible on the following topics:

> bringing up children (Eph 6:1–4; Prov 13:24)
> dealing with a spouse (Eph 5:22–28,33; 1 Pet 3:1–7; Col 3:18,19)
> employees (Eph 6:5–8; Col 3:22–25)
> employers (Eph 6:9; Col 4:1)
> authority (1 Tim 2:2, 1 Pet 2:13,14; Rom 13:1–7)
> money (Mk 12:14–17; Deut 14:22,23; Prov 11:28; Jer 17:11; Matt 13:22; 6:19–21)
> work (Matt 10:10; 2 Tim 2:15; 2 Thess 3:10)
> neighbours (1 Pet 2:12; Lk 10:27–37; Rom 13:9)

It is obvious, therefore, that to be able to get your objective right—of pleasing God—you must know or learn from the Maker's Manual what pleases God generally and specifically.

There will be times, of course, when there does not seem to be clear guidance from the Maker's Manual to cover the situation that you are in or how you should act; in such cases you should act as you feel that his Son would act. If you get this right then you are bound to please God. To get it right, you also need to know from your study of the Maker's Manual not only how Jesus Christ did act during his life on earth, but the kind of person he is and therefore how he would treat a certain person or situation. In other words, your objective in all your dealings with people should not be to change them or their actions, but to please God in all your dealings towards them, leaving the changing for God to do.

This does not mean to say that you must not hope and pray that people or situations will change (Jas 5:13), but change must not be your overriding objective. St Paul tells us 'Don't worry about anything; instead, pray about everything; tell God your needs and don't forget to thank him for his answers. If you do this, you will experience God's peace, which is far more wonderful than the human mind can understand. His peace will keep your thoughts and your hearts quiet and at rest as you trust in Christ Jesus' (Phil 4:6,7, Living Bible).

If your objective is to do your best, to do what is right and above all to please God, leaving the changes to him, then you cannot fail because of someone else's actions. You are in charge, you are always in control, and achieving your objective is in your hands. You need never get frustrated, because you need never fail; you need never become anxious or suffer from effects of stress when you have not been able to change a stressor, because change is in God's hands.

We saw in Chapter 11 that if you get your thinking, attitudes and actions right in this way you will be surprised how often the person or situation does change without you trying to bring about the change. In that same chapter we gave a few illustrative examples.

Your objective with a wayward or difficult spouse should not be to change them, because you have no ultimate control over this. Instead you must please God in all your dealings with your spouse, doing your best to be a good husband or wife. The Manual is quite explicit about this. If you know what will please God, then you may not even have to amend what you are doing, but only the reason for doing it. Remember the reason for your behaviour is not to bring about change, but in order to do right, and so that God will be pleased. Any change in your spouse is not your responsibility in the end, because you have no control over him or her.

At work, your objective should not be promotion, but to please God in all things you do and in all your relationships at work. The Manual spells out what your actions and attitudes at work should be; if you follow these actions and adopt these attitudes, then you will please God and will never fail, even if promotion never comes.

In dealing with a difficult child your objective should not be to change the child, but to do what is right, to do your best as a parent, and to please God in all your dealings with the child. You must be very clear about what will please God about bringing up a child and disciplining a child and you must put these actions into practice—not to change the child, but because it is right and in order to please God: leave the changing to God. In this case, as in many others, it is not enough that you do the right things. You may carry out all biblical instructions to do with bringing up a child—but if you are doing them in order to change the child, then you can be heading for disaster. Your whole attitude should be, 'I am doing these things, behaving in this way, to please God, irrespective of the outcome. I will leave the outcome, the changing of the child, to God.

When I toured a number of cities contributing to MARC Europe's Stress and Spirituality seminars, I found that one of the biggest stressors in the ministry at this time is the church growth movement. If your objective as a minister of religion or pastor is for your church to grow, then if it grows, you feel good. If for any reason (a population shift, the arrival of a young, dynamic minister in a church down the road) numbers begin to dwindle, then you try harder, work harder, even pray harder. The harder you try and the more anxious you get, the worse things become. You even begin putting people off because of your anxious manner. Eventually you have a nervous breakdown. You have made yourself very vulnerable because, in the end, you have no control over whether your church grows or not. God has said *'I will build my church'* (Matt 16:18).

There is nothing wrong with wanting God's church to grow. There is nothing wrong with praying for it, nothing wrong with doing all you can to encourage growth. But your objective in all your church work should be to do your best, to do what is right and to please God. The increase is in his hands. If he chooses to make your church grow, then that is wonderful. But if for his purposes he chooses to make another church grow, then that is wonderful too. As long as your only objective has been to please God, then you will not have failed. You need not get depressed, have a nervous breakdown, or develop other effects of stress.

Praising God

If you can look on everything that happens to you as having a purpose, and feel assured that good will come out of it, then you are less likely to suffer from strain when faced with stressors. Christian belief is that all that happens to us is working for our good 'if we love God' (Rom 8:28). If your faith in God and in his son, Jesus Christ, assures you that God is in control of everything, then should you not thank God in all circumstances, whether *you* think they are 'good' or 'bad'?

This is the next principle for successful living—that we should thank God for whatever happens to us. This advice may seem strange, but it is what the Maker's Manual says we should do (1 Thess 5:16–18). If we look at it a little more closely, we may begin to see that it does make some sense.

You have probably been taught that you should thank

God for the good things that happen to you—and that is right—for food, clothes, a home, a job, family, friends, for protection, for guidance, for unexpected blessings that come to you. Most of us have sung the hymn 'Praise my soul the King of Heaven' at some time in our lives. But what about the 'bad' things that happen to you or to others—the loss of a job, loss of a loved one, a tragedy in the family, failure in business, failure at college or in examinations? You tend to think that these have come not from God, who is a loving Father, but from other, possibly evil, people, or from the devil himself. Often your first reaction is to ask God to change the circumstances—to give you back what you have lost or to make it better. But wait a minute! The Maker's Manual says that God is all-powerful, that he is sovereign, he can do anything, and he is stronger and more powerful than the evil one or all evil itself. So, either he has actually caused the bad things to happen to you or he has allowed it to happen to you.

The Bible also states that everything that happens to you is for your good—that God has your good at heart (Rom 8:28). So, if you accept these ideas, why then do you immediately ask God to change what happens to you when you feel it to be bad, and why do you thank him only for the good things?

Is it not more logical and sensible to thank and praise him for everything, even the 'bad', that happens to you? After all, he is at the back of it and he means it for your good. Granted, sometimes it does not seem to make too much sense to praise God for things that appear nothing but disastrous to you, but the real logic is that you should, and the Maker's Manual says that you should.

There is a temptation to go part of the way and to 'accept' what is happening and to put up with it. Perhaps you grin and bear it, or at least grit your teeth; perhaps

APPLYING GOD'S PRINCIPLES

you look for the silver lining in the bad event or circumstance, trying to work out what good may come of it. Then you say to yourself, 'Ah, if that good comes of it, then I will be able to praise God.' But that is not the instruction. You have to praise him for everything, even when you do not know and cannot see what good could possibly come of it. Do you really believe that he knows best, or don't you?

If you can bring yourself to praise God for everything, even the worst of happenings, then two big things begin to happen. First, your spirits do rise. Despite dreadful circumstances, many people have found that when they start praising God, they begin to feel strangely at peace and less depressed and dejected. Secondly, circumstances often do change quite rapidly. In fact, they often change more rapidly when you praise than when you were praying hard for change. When you acknowledge that circumstances are in God's hands, and that he does know what is best, it seems that God can then quite quickly work through what is in his mind to do. Many people can vouch for this, too.

So the instruction is to thank God for everything, even the bad things, whether you can see any good coming of it or not. Believe that everything has a purpose for your good. Only after you have thanked him should you begin to think of asking whether he wants to go on and change the circumstances. If you feel that he does, then it is right for you to pray that he will do so—with the proviso that even if God does not change things in the way you would like, still you will go on thanking him.

Then you will feel your spirits rise; do not be surprised when the circumstances change, perhaps in the way you would like, but perhaps in some quite different and unexpected way.

Further reading

1. *Basic Principles of Biblical Counselling.* Lawrence J. Crabb. Marshall, Morgan & Scott, 1985.
2. *Second Honeymoon.* Dave and Joyce Ames. Kingsway, Eastbourne, 1986.
3. *Marriage as God Intended.* Selwyn Hughes. Kingsway, Eastbourne, 1983.
4. *God's Time, God's Money.* Sir Fred Catherwood. Hodder & Stoughton, London, 1987.
5. *Prison to Praise.* Merlin Carothers. Hodder & Stoughton, London.

Part Four

Making It Work

21
A CHANGE OF LIFE

You now have the knowledge not only to cope with pressures, to prevent and manage stress, but to live positively and successfully. The secrets outlined in Part Three may be new to you, and you may not have any experience of trying to apply them. On the other hand, you may have known the secrets for a long time but have never really wanted to try them out—or perhaps you have been afraid in case they don't work, or have tried and tried again, unsuccessfully, to make them work.

If you approach it in the wrong way, it is difficult to make yourself change your whole outlook and lifestyle in order to increase your resistance to stress. If you try in the wrong way and keep trying, you will fail and will wear yourself out. You will not make yourself less vulnerable, but because of your effort and failure, and the guilt attached to failing, you may even make yourself more vulnerable and end up suffering from effects of stress.

However, you are about to learn the surest way of actually wanting to apply the secrets, and then how to have the ability and power within you to put them into practice. My wife and I have put this to the test and many people who have attended our seminars have been able to start living a richly satisfying life in a way they had only dreamed of.

The key, as you have seen thus far, lies in your soul

and in your thinking, feelings and behaviour being as God intends them to be. How do you change your thinking, feelings and behaviour? The answer quite simply is that *you don't*. You can try, but it will not work consistently. Nor does God want to help you to change them. You can ask God to help you to change, and this may have a limited and temporary effect. But even this is not the surest way—and it is not what God recommends. What then is the secret?

God, in the person of his Holy Spirit, offers to come to live in your soul supernaturally. (He is already in your spirit if you are born again.) If this happens, then you will find yourself thinking as he does, feeling as he does and acting as he does. However, this can happen only if you give up control of your soul. That includes the way you want to think (and the way you have always thought, both consciously and unconsciously), the way you feel, the decisions you make and the way you act and behave.

In other words, you can exchange your life for his. St Paul says 'I have been crucified with Christ, and I no longer live, but Christ lives in me' (Gal 2:20).

It can work like this for you.

Step one

Make over control of your life to God. We have found that the surest way of doing this is to take pen and paper and write a letter to Jesus.

Dear Jesus,
I give up my rights to the ways I think and feel and behave.

Then make a list of all that goes to make up your life, the good and the bad, your assets—talents, work, money, house, possessions, your wife/husband, children, friends, health, your future, and so on. Then list your debits—

fears, anxieties, depression, illnesses, the past, your failures, doubts and confusions, etc.

Take some time over the letter. Do it prayerfully, asking God that he will show you the things that should be included. Having completed your list, date and sign it. It is tempting simply to do the transaction in your mind, to pray in general terms that God will take control of your life, but we have found that it has a much greater effect in those who actually write the letter. Putting pen to paper will make you be more definite and specific about the details; signing it makes it more tangible and binding. So we would urge you to take the time and the effort to write the letter. It is the most important document that you will ever write and sign.

Having completed the letter, you have a number of options as to what to do with it. You can read it over with a trusted friend: for some people this makes it more meaningful. Others prefer to tear it up or burn it. Others prefer to put it away safely in case they want to review it, remind themselves of what they have relinquished, or perhaps add to it in the future. You can do with it whatever suits you. The important thing is that you have written it.

Step two

The Holy Spirit must be asked to fill the vacuum in your soul left by your self-abdication. You can do this yourself, by praying,

> Lord Jesus, I have put in writing the fact that I have relinquished my rights to my life including my soul life. I wish to empty my soul of all my own thinking, feelings, will and behaviour. I now ask that you will fill my soul with your Holy Spirit.
>
> I want to exchange my life for yours. Amen.

Alternatively you can ask someone—a Christian friend, pastor or leader—to pray that you will be filled by the Holy Spirit. This is not necessary, but you may consider it more real if someone else prays for you.

If you pray in this way or if you are prayed for, and believe that it will happen, then it will, and you can wait for the changes which may surprise you.

Although we have separated steps one and two from the initial transaction of being born again, ideally they should follow hot on its footsteps. We have illustrated these processes diagramatically below (based on Charles Solomon's 'Wheel Diagram' in *Handbook to Happiness*).[1]

1. Our original state

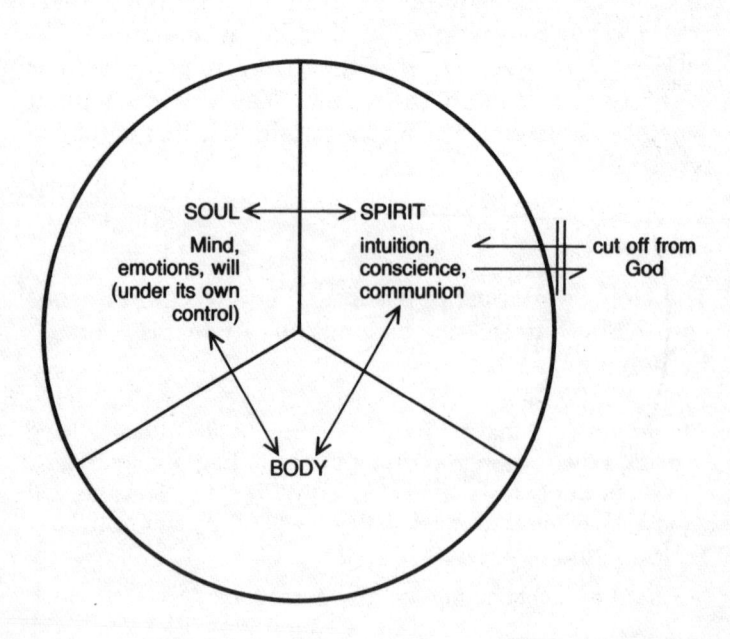

```
        SOUL ←——→ SPIRIT
        Mind,        intuition,         ⇤╫   cut off from
     emotions, will  conscience, ——        God
     (under its own  communion
        control)

              BODY
```

A CHANGE OF LIFE 153

2. *After being born again*

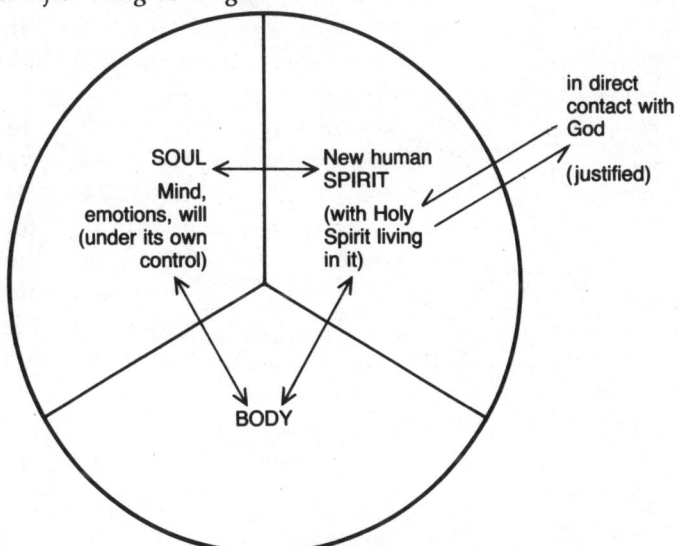

- SOUL — Mind, emotions, will (under its own control)
- New human SPIRIT (with Holy Spirit living in it) — in direct contact with God (justified)
- BODY

3. *After writing the letter and asking to be filled with the Spirit*

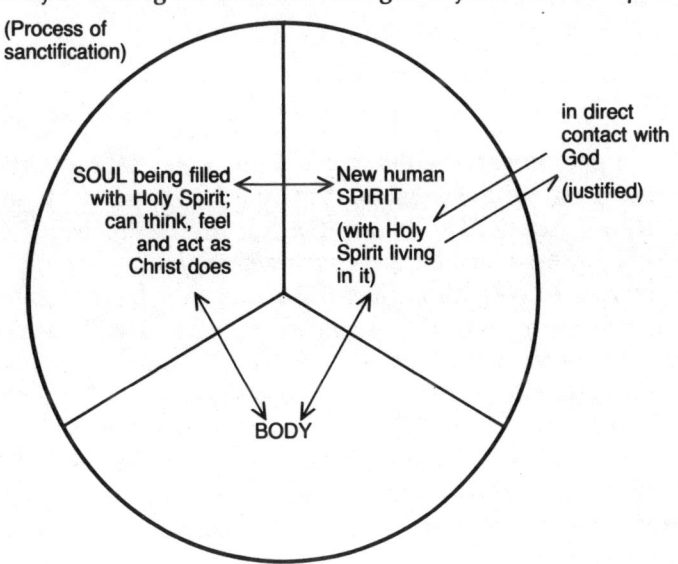

(Process of sanctification)

- SOUL being filled with Holy Spirit; can think, feel and act as Christ does
- New human SPIRIT (with Holy Spirit living in it) — in direct contact with God (justified)
- BODY

4. Final state

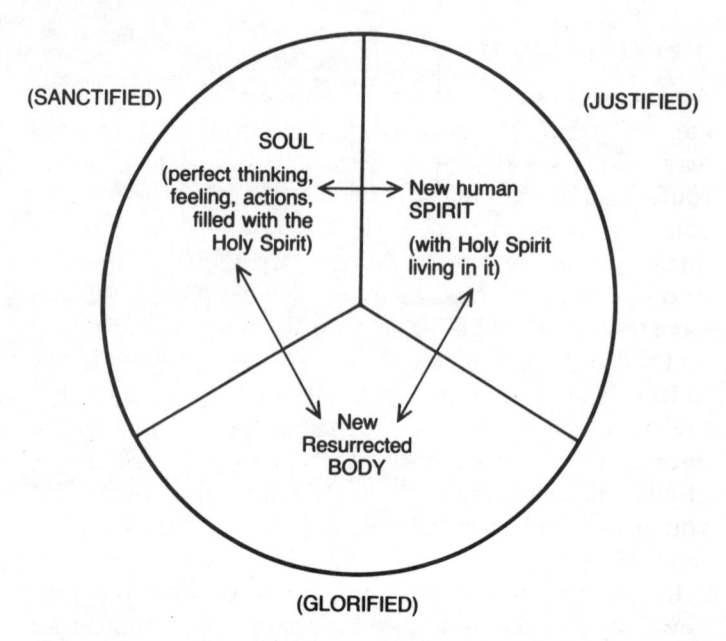

(SANCTIFIED)

(JUSTIFIED)

SOUL
(perfect thinking, feeling, actions, filled with the Holy Spirit)

New human SPIRIT
(with Holy Spirit living in it)

New Resurrected BODY

(GLORIFIED)

I hope you can see the tremendous potential not only for coping with stressors, but for living life as your designer means it to be, to the full (Jn 10:10), because Christ—God—himself now lives within you.

Instead of your mind thinking about things, perhaps in a confused or defeated or depressed way, it will be his mind at work in you (1 Cor 2:16), and he is the source of all wisdom and truth. You will have his feelings (because you have his thinking) and he is never depressed or anxious. You will make decisions and act as he does. He never fails or gets things wrong, and he is all-powerful. This is not too good to be true! It can happen to you. You will not be disappointed.

You need not suffer from the effects of stress. You can live successfully if you function as he has designed you to.

A word of warning

At any time you can take back control of any part of your life. For example, you may begin to think in a worried way, and this may give rise to feelings of anxiety, which could lead on to effects of stress. You may know that you are taking back control, but often it can happen insidiously and almost without you realising it. Anxiety or other 'bad' feelings are a sure warning sign that you have taken back some control, and that you are not filled by the Holy Spirit as you once were. The solution is not to try harder to change things or yourself, or to look for involved and complicated reasons for what is going wrong. Instead you should once again give up all control of your life and your soul, and ask the Holy Spirit to fill you again. Let him release his thoughts and feelings and power in you.

In fact you should start each phase of your life, each new project, every new day, by giving up control of your soul (this is sometimes called 'dying to self') and asking the Holy Spirit to take charge. Jesus said that daily we should 'take up our cross' (Lk 9:23): I do not believe that this means that you should take up life's problems and burdens and struggle under them. Rather it means that you should die to yourself again: in Christ's day, anyone who took up a cross to carry it was doomed to die thereafter. Jesus also said, 'If you insist on saving your life, you will lose it. Only those who throw away their lives for my sake and for the sake of the Good News will ever know what it means to really live' (Mk 8:35, Living Bible).

You can see that there will be setbacks in overcoming

stressors and living successfully, but only when you take back control, either defiantly or almost unwittingly. Throughout the rest of your life this will be an ongoing process as far as your soul is concerned—a process known as 'sanctification'. This process will be completed only upon death. You will see that in the diagrams on p. 153 we have inserted 'Sanctification' as a process. Being 'Justified' happens instantly when you accept Christ's death to restore you from your state of spiritual death, and from going your own way. Similarly, you will instantly be given a new body on Christ's return to earth, which is known as 'Resurrection'.

A word of promise

The more you learn to leave control of your life to Jesus, and the more you remain filled with the Holy Spirit, the more successfully you will live, and the less you will be affected by stressors.

Jesus himself promised this when he said, 'I have told you all this so that you will have peace of heart and mind. Here on earth you will have many trials and sorrows (stressors), but take courage, I have overcome the world' (Jn 16:33, Living Bible).

Note

1. Solomon, C. R. *Handbook to Happiness* Living Studies (Tyndale House, Illinois, 1985).

FURTHER RESOURCES

All the resources described on the following pages are available from:

> Stress and Life Trust (SALT)
> The Istana
> Freezeland Lane
> Bexhill-on-Sea
> East Sussex, TN39 5JD
>
> Telephone: (0424) 219133

- *Stress Facts and Action Plan Pack*

  In a handy pack with questionnaires and self assessments. The whole-person approach to stress prevention and management. Christian beliefs applied to the latest from stress research by Dr Bill Munro. Helpful for Christians but also designed to appeal to others.

- *Information about Counselling and Seminars*

  Seminars—Christian or secular—for churches, Christians, outreach, organisations and industry on prevention and management of stress, and living and working successfully.

- *Relaxation Tapes*

- *Teaching Tapes*

  On the prevention and management of stress, and living and working successfully.

Beat Stress — A 30 Day Programme
by Dr Bill and Frances Munro
(Published by Harper Collins 1993)

From the Foreword by Jennifer Rees Larcombe

This book was such a relief to me because it does not condemn us for being human and feeling pressures. But . . . it not only sympathises; it reminds us that as Christians we do not have to be crushed and destroyed. There is a way we can cope with the stress of life and it goes on to show us how, in a simple and straightforward way.

In this book, Bill and Frances break down the concepts they teach in their seminars into simple daily steps. When you are feeling stressed up to the eye-balls the last thing you want to do is read a book on the subject! But the joy of this book is that you don't have to read it! At least, not all at once! I found it so helpful just being able to go through it a few pages each day; giving myself time to re-think my priorities and absorb all the practical tips and suggestions.

Sometimes when life is really being tough it is hard to pray and you can't seem to think where to look in the Bible to find the help you need. So the beautiful little prayers and relevant verses for each day are a very good idea indeed. I also loved the humour! They say laughter is the best medicine and some of the stories and statements in the book made me weep with laughter—a real tonic.

It would be a great shame if people did not read this book until they were beginning to suffer from stress. Prevention is better than cure so I believe it is a must for all busy people. While it is an excellent step by step method of beating stress it is an equally excellent step by step guide to becoming a whole human being, fit and healthy in body, mind and spirit.